PRAYERS IN CHURCH

To David Cavendish Rea,
Commissioned as
Diocesan Reader in
Dublin & Glendalough
on Advent III. Dec 15th 1991.
Read + Mark Well &
Be a faithful Dispenser
of the Word of the Lord.

✝ Carlisle

PRAYERS IN CHURCH

A new collection of occasional prayers arranged for present-day use

Edited by

JOHN CONACHER, Dip. Th.

OXFORD UNIVERSITY PRESS

1987

Oxford University Press, Walton Street, Oxford OX2 6DP
Oxford New York Toronto
Delhi Bombay Calcutta Madras Karachi
Petaling Jaya Singapore Hong Kong Tokyo
Nairobi Dar es Salaam Cape Town
Melbourne Auckland
and associated companies in
Beirut Berlin Ibadan Nicosia

Oxford is a trade mark of Oxford University Press

British Library Cataloguing in Publication Data
Prayers in church: a new collection of occasional prayers arranged for present-day use.
1. Church of Ireland—Prayer-books and devotions—English
I. Conacher, John Roy Hamilton
264'.03   BX5535
ISBN 0-19-143501-5

Set by Wyvern Typesetting Limited, Bristol
Printed in Great Britain

CONTENTS

FOREWORD

THE issue of alternative prayer books in modern English, both in the Church of England and in the Church of Ireland, has prompted a number of spiritual leaders to compile collections of prayers in like idiom. In many cases old prayers have been modernized, but there has been a welcome appearance of new prayers which will breathe a new spirit into worship.

The present collection contains many such new prayers which have been arranged in a methodical fashion—which will be a great help to the busy parish clergyman or lay reader, seeking prayers for regular Sunday services and special occasions. The compiler is a licensed lay reader in the Church of Ireland, and so has that church very much in mind in the choices he has made. However, I am sure that this book will have a wider appeal.

It is a great privilege to have been asked to commend this work, which I gladly do. I know all the years of personal devotion which lie behind this varied compilation. I hope the clergy and laity will find it a useful addition to their devotional bookshelves.

JOHN W. ARMSTRONG
*formerly Archbishop of Armagh and
Primate of all Ireland 1980–6*

PREFACE

As an ordinary member of a congregation, I have long believed
that worship by Christian people in today's world needs to be
expressed in today's language. As a lay reader, I have often spent
much of my preparation time for taking services in the search for
occasional prayers written in language that would seem relevant
and natural for those whose worship I would be responsible for
leading. As a bookseller, I have seen how eager a demand there
has been from clergy and lay readers for books of prayers in
modern speech for liturgical use. As a member of the Church of
Ireland, I have been aware of the extent to which, in varying
degrees, the books that have appeared in recent times have not
been fully attuned to the circumstances of that Church.

So it was that I accepted the invitation from Oxford University
Press to edit a new collection of occasional prayers, suitable for
use today, alongside the Alternative Prayer Book 1984 autho-
rized by the Church of Ireland. Its title *Prayers in Church* will
make it clear that its main intent is not for private devotions but
to meet the needs of public worship.

This was the genesis of the book. What then has been the plan
for its construction, and the materials from which it has been
assembled? The main feature of its plan has been the provision of
a selection of prayers for the topics prescribed for each Sunday
and major feast set out in the Alternative Prayer Book (APB); of
the seven sections in the book, by far the largest (that entitled
The Church's Year) will take its user right through the liturgical
year by the same path as does the APB. Whilst many of the
prayers from tried-and-tested collections were readily available
as its materials (though often with adaptation for the Church of
Ireland or for the use of modern speech, or both), copyright
restrictions unexpectedly required me to contribute a significant
proportion of original prayers.

An important impulse for me in preparing this original
material was Archbishop Lord Coggan's *Prayers of the New
Testament*, in which he works thoughtfully through all the
passages in which a prayer is expressed. I have used this book at
intervals over many years, and a recent re-reading made me ask
myself why, if all these prayers are there in the Bible itself, we do
not use them more. This question itself provides the main reason
why so much of the material in *Prayers in Church* is drawn from
the Bible. A second reason derives from the fact that much of the
content of the Book of Common Prayer, and of the APB, is taken
from Scripture; to be consistent then, as many of the occasional

prayers as possible should also be derived from the Bible. A third reason relates to my own conviction of the supremacy of the Bible over all other written material; a congregation is more likely to be praying with the mind of Christ if it is using the words of Scripture rather than words of mine.

One particular part of this book needs some explanation. As a lay reader, who customarily is not expected to use the 'Benediction' at the close of a service, I have built up my personal collection of portions of Scripture which I have myself found suitable for use as the concluding words of a service. These form the 'Valedictions' printed as numbers 244 to 263 inclusive.

Since the APB uses the text of the New International Version (NIV) translation of the Bible, the wording of the Scripture-related prayers has been aligned in almost every case to that of the NIV.

I have been immensely impressed by the time and care Archbishop Armstrong has taken in going through the manuscript of this book, and am indeed grateful to him for the suggestions he has made for improvements. I appreciate, too, the courtesy of holders of copyright who have allowed their material to be reproduced, and especially when they have consented to some changes of detail in the form in which their prayers have previously been printed.

At the back of this book the user will find more than he might expect in the form of indexes. In addition to an index of the topics referred to in the prayers, he will also find an index of Scripture allusions, and a table setting out the use through the year of the Bible passages printed *in extenso* in the APB. A further table shows the dates over a number of years ahead on which fall the Sundays of the liturgical year, and, consequently, on which these Bible passages are appointed to be used.

May this book play a part in the fulfilment among us of the prayer that Paul used: 'I have not stopped giving thanks for you, remembering you in my prayers. I keep asking that the God of our Lord Jesus Christ, the glorious Father, may give you the Spirit of wisdom and revelation, so that you may know him better.' Ephesians 1: 16–17 (NIV).

Bell's Hill   JOHN CONACHER
Limavady
County Londonderry
February 1987

THE CHURCH'S YEAR

HONOURING THE CREATOR   1

We praise you, God almighty, for the power you have shown in
creating the world. We thank you for your love in redeeming us
from sin and creating us anew in Christ. Grant us strength to
honour you all our lives, both in worship and in witness, for
Jesus Christ's sake.

R. C. Thorp

LIGHT FOR GOD'S WORLD   2

Lord God, of all-surpassing power,
    we bring our worship to you,
        who as Creator said
            'Let light shine out of darkness';
    we bring our thanks and praise to you,
        who in redemption
            made your light shine in our hearts;
    we offer our own selves to you,
        whose Son suffered death
            that his life may be revealed in us.
Glory in heaven and on earth be to
    God the Creator,
    God the Saviour and
    God the Holy Spirit.

(Gen. 1: 3; 2 Cor. 4: 4–10)   *J. C.*

3   OUR IMPERFECT PERCEPTION

Almighty Creator, we praise you for your majesty and power,
    of which we perceive only a part,
      as we contemplate the immensity of the night sky,
        the unmoving mountains and
        the expanse of the seas.
We praise you for the endless diversity
          of your skills and care,
    of which we know so little,
      while we continue to learn more
        about the tiny creatures you have made and
        about the complexity of our own bodies.
We sorrow at the pain and disorder in your world
    that results from man's sin.
And we pray that you will hasten that day
    when the creation itself will be
      liberated from bondage and
      brought into the glorious freedom of the children of God;
      through Christ our Lord.

(Ps. 8; Rom. 8: 19–21)

                                    J. C.

4   A SIMPLE 'GENERAL THANKSGIVING'

Heavenly Father, we thank you
    for all your great goodness towards us.
We thank you for the world, and all the good things in it;
    for the sky above us, and the earth beneath our feet;
    for the changing seasons, the sunshine and the rain;
    for our homes, our relations and friends.
Help us not to take your goodness for granted,
    but constantly to give you thanks,
      not only by what we say,
      but by the way we try to please you
      in everything we do,
        through Jesus Christ our Lord.

John Eddison

8TH SUNDAY BEFORE CHRISTMAS   The Fall

THE HOUR WHEN WE ARE TEMPTED   5

Lord, we need your help in the hour when the evil one
    tempts us to reach out for what seems
        pleasing to the eye
        or desirable for our self-esteem.
Recall us then to the way of your commandments
    by the voice of your Holy Spirit,
  and give us strength that we may continue
    Christ's faithful soldiers and servants to our life's end.

(Gen. 3: 6)   *J. C.*

LOVE THAT CAN BE SEEN   6

Lord God, you have declared to us how we know what
love is—that Jesus Christ laid down his life for us.

Help us to have that same love, expressed not just with
words or tongue, but in actions and in truth; help us to know
that we have passed from death to life because we love our
brothers.

May those who watch us see in what we do the marks of
the children of God, and turn from the evil one to your truth,
having hearts at rest in your presence;
    through our Saviour Jesus Christ.

(1 John 3: 11–19)   *J. C.*

7TH SUNDAY BEFORE CHRISTMAS
The Election of God's People: Abraham

THE FAITH THAT OBEYS   7

Almighty God, who told Abraham to leave home and to find his
security not in circumstances but in obedience, help us to obey
the commands which we have heard, to do what we know to be
right, and to leave the consequences to you; for Jesus' sake.

(Gen. 12: 1)   *J. Wheatley Price*

8   FAITH IN THE PROMISES

We praise you Lord for your loving grace
    by which men receive
        the righteousness that comes by faith.
We pray that by your continuance of this grace
    we may not waver through unbelief in your promises,
    but instead may be fully persuaded
        that you have power
    to do what you have promised to us,
        for whose sins Jesus our Lord
            was delivered over to death, and
        for whose justification he was raised to life.

(Rom. 4: 13, 20–5;   J. C.

9   THANKSGIVING FOR SALVATION AND DISCIPLESHIP

Father, we thank you
    for the gift of Jesus Christ, to be the Way, the Truth,
        and the Life;
    for the love which moved him to endure the cross for us
        and for all mankind;
    for the victory of his resurrection and the glory of his
        ascension;
    for the outpouring of the Holy Spirit,
        and the witness of the church through many
            centuries;
    for the encouragement of our growing awareness that we
        are all one in Christ Jesus;
    for the blessings received in belonging to each other in
        the fellowship of the Holy Spirit;
    for the privilege of being called
            to discipleship of Jesus Christ,
        to bear witness
            to his eternal presence and his saving power.
For all these joyful gifts, thanks be to you, O God.

(John 14: 6)   *Alan C. Warren*

6TH SUNDAY BEFORE CHRISTMAS
The Promise of Redemption: Moses

SPEAKING WITH GOD AND SPEAKING TO MEN 10

When your children, O God, have no freedom and are oppressed by tyranny, grant to them leaders like Moses: men who speak with you face to face; men who communicate with the rulers of the land.

And by your outstretched hand and holy arm, O Lord, lead your people into liberty by ways which you shall choose,
    through Christ our Lord.

(Ex. 33: 11)   *Dick Williams*

PREPARATION FOR SERVICE 11

Strengthen, Lord, your servants whom you are now preparing and training for some great work, which is perhaps still unknown to them but which in your wisdom and sovereignty you plan for them.

Give them a steadily deepening experience of yourself, a clearer perception of their own selves, a growing understanding of your word, and a fuller trust in your love and power.

Grant that, in the day when you open before them the door of your purpose, they may step out in humble faith in Jesus Christ, the Way, the Truth, and the Life.

(John 14: 6)   *J. C.*

5TH SUNDAY BEFORE CHRISTMAS
(Sunday next before Advent)   The Remnant of Israel

12   OUR INDEBTEDNESS

O God our Father, we thank you for inspiring
    Hebrew writers to give us the Bible, and
    Hebrew prophets to prepare the way of Christ.
We thank you for the Jewish disciples
        who were the first missionaries
                and preachers of the Good News.
We thank you above all for Jesus, your Son,
        who was born to a Jewish mother.
Help us to repay so great a debt
        by doing all we can to send the message of Jesus
                back to the Jewish people
      who first gave it to us,
      and yet today know so little of Jesus and his love;
        for his name's sake.

Walter Barker

13   THE PROPHETIC MINISTRY

Lord, send us prophets in the Church today,
    as in the days of old,
    to make known your living truth
      in the power of the Holy Spirit.
Give them a clear vision of your purpose
    for the life of the world;
    enable them to speak the Word with all boldness;
    and through their voice recall your people
      to simpler discipleship,
      to holier living,
      and to more dedicated service,
    for the glory of our Lord Jesus Christ.

Frank Colquhoun

4TH SUNDAY BEFORE CHRISTMAS
(Advent)   The Advent Hope

WAITING FOR HIS COMING   14

Lord Jesus, Redeemer and Judge of_~~men~~_, ^{all}
  who came to save us from our sins:
you have taught us that you will come again
  to take account of your servants and
  to reward faithful service.
Help us to live as ~~men~~ who wait for their master,
  alert and ready for action,
  with lamps burning, maintaining a good witness,
that we may not be ashamed before you at your coming
  but may enter into your eternal joy.

(Matt. 25: 19–21; Luke 12: 35–8)   *Frank Colquhoun*

READY AND RESPONSIBLE   15

Help us, Lord Jesus, to live as your servants,
        ready for your return.
May we rest our hope and confidence in you alone,
    and be ready to help others
        joyfully to meet you in your glory.

(Matt. 25: 1–13)   *J. C.*

3RD SUNDAY BEFORE CHRISTMAS
(Advent 2)   The Word of God in the Old Testament

LEARNING AND OBEYING GOD'S WILL   16

Lord God, you have given us your holy word
        to be a lamp to our feet and a light for our path.
Grant us all your Holy Spirit,
        that we may from your word learn your will,
        and may, by his help, frame our lives in obedience to it.
So may your name be honoured,
        and our faith increased,
            through Jesus Christ our Lord.

(Ps. 119: 105)   *Edward Dering*

17   OBEYING THE BIBLE

We thank you, Lord, for the many ways you have revealed your mind and declared your counsel to the hearts of men in all ages. In particular we thank you for the holy scriptures in which we learn all we need to know of your love for men and your purpose for history.

Help us so to know your word that we may understand it, so to love it that we may obey it, and so to obey it that we may cause it to be heard, loved, and obeyed throughout creation; for the sake of Jesus Christ our Lord.

Dick Williams

18   THANKSGIVING FOR THE BIBLE

Thank you, Lord, for the Bible:
    for its ability to give to us each day
        new vision and new power;
    for its capacity to reach to the roots of inner life
        and to refresh them;
    for its authority to enter mind and spirit
        and fashion them anew;
    for its power to beget new life
        and to sustain it.
For all this, we give you thanks and praise,
    through Jesus Christ our Lord.

Dick Williams

19   LIVING OUT THE GOSPEL

May the Spirit of the Lord be upon us that we may preach good news to the poor, proclaim freedom for the prisoners, and recovery of sight for the blind; that we may release the oppressed, and proclaim the year of the Lord's favour; according to the example of Christ and by his grace.

(Luke 4: 18–19)   *Dick Williams*

2ND SUNDAY BEFORE CHRISTMAS
(Advent 3)   The Forerunner

AMBASSADORS FOR CHRIST   20

O God, your gospel has the strength to set free those who are entangled and imprisoned by their own sins. Grant power to every member of your church that, being ambassadors for Christ, they may so speak of him—crucified, risen, and alive today—that many may come to share in the glorious freedom of your children; through the power of his name and for the sake of his name.

(2 Cor. 5: 20)   *C. Idle*

JUDGEMENT AND GRACE   21

Lord God, as you sent your servant John
    to prepare men for the first coming
      of your Son Jesus Christ,
  we pray that you will impel your church today
    to declare and demonstrate
          before an unbelieving world
      that you have standards of right and wrong
        by which men will be judged; and also
     to make known your grace,
        by which there is now no condemnation
          for those who are in Christ Jesus.

(Luke 1: 17; Rom. 8: 1)   *J. C.*

WITNESSES TO CHRIST   22

We thank you, Father, for Jesus Christ our Lord, and for giving his church the work of spreading the gospel and of announcing his death and resurrection.

Be with all who are his witnesses: missionaries in other countries, ministers and other workers here at home, youth leaders and teachers in day school and Sunday School, and all Christians everywhere. Make and keep them faithful to you, true to your message, and full of love for the world and its people, for Jesus Christ's sake.

Anon.

SUNDAY BEFORE CHRISTMAS
(Advent 4)   The Annunciation

23   A MODERN VERSION OF THE BIDDING PRAYER FOR A
SERVICE OF LESSONS AND CAROLS

Good Christian friends, at this Christmas time let us prepare ourselves to hear again, in word and song, the good tidings of God's redeeming love made known to us in the birth of the Holy Child of Bethlehem; and with the angelic host let us give glory to God in the highest.

But first let us pray for the needs of the whole world: for peace and goodwill among all nations; for unity and brotherhood in this community and in our diocese of . . . . . .; for love and harmony in our families and our homes; and for a blessing on all children dear to us, and on loved ones absent from home.

Let us also remember at this time those for whom Christmas brings little joy: the poor and homeless, the hungry and destitute, the unemployed, the sick and those who mourn; and all victims of tyranny, cruelty, violence and oppression.

Lastly, let us remember with thanksgiving those who shared our Christmasses in years gone by and who now rejoice in the greater light of God's heavenly kingdom. To their company, and to the fellowship of all the citizens above, may God in his mercy bring us all.

Let us bring together all our prayers in the words our Saviour Christ taught us:
'Our Father . . .'

Frank Colquhoun

24   PREPARATION FOR CHRISTMAS

Heavenly Father, how much the glory of that first Christmas
consisted in
the richness of your gift to mankind and
the simplicity of Mary's trust in your word!
In all our busy-ness at Christmas-time,
help us to prepare ourselves humbly
to rejoice in the gift of new life in Jesus and
to hear and receive your word.

So may we know the true joy,
    in our homes and
    in our hearts,
        through Christ our Saviour.

(John 3: 16; Luke 1: 38)   *J. C.*

CHRISTMAS GIVING   25

Help us this Christmas-time, good Lord,
    to take more joy
        in giving than in receiving,
        in loving than in being loved.
May the true spirit of this joyful season
    fill our hearts and our homes, and
    overflow to everyone we meet;
        for love of Jesus, our Saviour.

(Acts 20: 35)   *Beryl Bye*

A FAMILY CHRISTMAS   26

O God, we shall be very busy over Christmas, and we know that we shall be tempted to forget its true meaning. Help us to conquer that temptation so that we all may share in our families the true joy of the Saviour's birth and may experience for ourselves our Emmanuel, God with us.

(Matt. 1: 23)   *Andrew Warner*

THE NEEDS OF THE POOR   27

Lord, as we make ready for Christmas amid so much affluence and abundance, keep us mindful of the poverty-stricken peoples of the world, the vast multitude who at this very time lack the bare necessities of life.

    Through the gifts we offer for their relief may we show something of our gratitude for all that you have given us; and may our gifts be acceptable through him who for our sake became poor and was born in a stable, Jesus our Saviour.

(2 Cor. 8: 9)   *Frank Colquhoun*

CHRISTMAS EVE

28   A BIDDING PRAYER

Let us pray for the church: that it may be as humble, as relevant, and as strong as the Lord who was born of Mary.

Let us pray for the world in all its achievements and yet in its need, in the glory of its creation and yet in the grief of its people: that it may look to God for help.

Let us pray that, as God stirred the wise men to follow the star and find Christ, so may we and all mankind be stirred to seek for the truth and to find the Saviour.

As God opened the heavens and spoke to summon the shepherds, let us pray that we and all men everywhere may look for God's word, and at its coming rise up and go where he shall direct.

And as God prepared Mary to be the mother of Jesus let us ask him to prepare our hearts and the hearts of all people to receive the Lord of glory; that in this glad and solemn season each heart might be a manger and each home a Bethlehem.

Dick Williams

29   THE EPHEMERAL AND THE ETERNAL

As Mary treasured up all the things that happened
          that first Christmas-time,
     and pondered them in her mind;
Help us, Lord Jesus,
     not to discard the real treasures with the tinsel.
May the Holy Spirit so wonderfully
          enlighten our minds,
          deepen our commitment and
          increase our love
     that we will rejoice in you and in your salvation
          this Christmas-time and
          in all the days ahead,
               till we come to your everlasting Kingdom.

(Luke 2: 19)   *J. C.*

THE SONG OF THE ANGELS
30

Lord Jesus, let us now offer you
  ourselves and
  our worship,
  that we may join from our hearts with the angels,
   praising God and saying
    'Glory to God in the highest,
    and on earth peace to men
    on whom his favour rests.'

(Luke 2: 13–14)
                J. C.

CHRISTMAS

WELCOME TO THE SAVIOUR
31

O God our Father, as we remember the birth of your Son Jesus
Christ, we welcome him with gladness as Saviour and pray that
there may always be room in our hearts and in our homes for him
to dwell with us as Lord.

            M. H. Botting's collection

THE MEANING OF IT ALL
32

We thank you, our heavenly Father,
  for the loveliness of the Christmas story:
 the child in the manger,
 the song of the angels,
 the homage of the shepherds,
 the tender love of Mary.
But most of all we thank you
  for the meaning of the Christmas story:
 that you loved the world so much
  that you gave your only Son,
   that all might live through him.
All praise and thanks be yours, O God,
   for so great a love,
   so great a gift,
   so great a Saviour,
    Jesus Christ our Lord.

              Frank Colquhoun

33   CHRISTMAS PEACE

Gracious God, we have heard again
>how the angels praised you by declaring both
your glory in the highest and
your peace on earth.
We pray for those who work for peace;
>for the statesmen of armed nations,
>for politicians in countries torn by dissent,
>for leaders in communities whose members are at
>>variance with one another.
May we, and all who belong to you,
>live as your chosen people,
>>a royal priesthood,
>>a holy nation
>declaring the praises of him who called us
>>out of darkness into his wonderful light;
>in the name of him who is
>>the Mighty God, the Prince of Peace.

(Luke 2: 14; 1 Pet. 2: 9; Isa. 9: 6)   *J. C.*

34   FAMILY CHRISTMAS

Our loving God, we reflect on Joseph and Mary; what must have made that first Christmas so wonderful for them was the coming of Jesus, even though they were far from their home at Nazareth.

Although many of us today will be gathered together as families, some of whose members have 'come home for Christmas', there will perhaps be others who are 'away from home'.

For each one, whether at home or away, may Jesus come among us; may we receive him as your gift, and know him as our friend.

So may this be a very happy Christmas for us all, in the joy of his name.

(Luke 2: 4–7)   *J. C.*

THE SAD, THE ILL, THE LONELY, THE POOR   **35**

Lord Jesus, as it was by your coming
    that joy was brought to Mary and Joseph,
      so may that same joy be brought ~~today~~
        to homes where people are sad, ill, lonely, or poor.
Stir us up, Lord, to our responsibilities ~~towards them.~~
Keep us from resisting your call to share with those in need
    the reality of our joy,
    the richness of your gifts and
    the good news of your coming.

J. C.

THE HOMELESS, THE HUNGRY, THE SUFFERING   **36**

Christ, born in a stable, give courage to the homeless.
Christ, who fled to Egypt, comfort the refugee.
Christ, who fasted in the desert, have mercy on the hungry.
Christ, who hung in torture on the cross, pity those in pain.
Christ, who died to save us, above all forgive our sin,
                    our greed,
                    our selfishness,
                    our unconcern.
Save us today, and use us in your loving purpose.

Simon Baynes

37   WHAT IT REALLY COST

Lord, keep us from forgetting some of the realities of that
    first Christmas—
    the oppression of an occupying army,
    the thoughtlessness of bureaucracy,
    the rigours of travel in winter,
    the selfishness at the inn,
    the squalor of the stable,
    the coarseness of the feeding trough,
    the pangs of childbirth,
    the cruelty of Herod,
    the years of exile in a foreign land.

As we remember all this, help us the more to understand
what it meant for him who was in very nature God to make
himself nothing, and then to become obedient to death, even
death on a cross.

At this Christmas time then let us not only bow our knees
and confess with our tongues that Jesus Christ is Lord, but let us
make over to him the love and the loyalty of our hearts, now and
for ever.

(Phil. 2: 7–10)   *J. C.*

NEW YEAR

---

38   YEARS PAST AND THE NEW YEAR

We praise you Lord for the wonderful ways in which
    you have given to repentant sinners
        pardon for all that is past, and
        a fresh start in life.
By faith in the name of Jesus may we have such faith
        now, and in the year ahead,
    that our lives shall be evidence
        of what you have done for us, and
        shall lead others also to experience
            your grace in forgiveness,
            your healing of body or mind, and

your power in life made new.
We ask it in the name of Jesus,
the name that is above every name.

(Acts 3: 16; Phil. 2: 9)   *J. C.*

THE NAME THAT IS ABOVE EVERY NAME   **39**

We praise you, heavenly Father, that you gave to your Son at his birth among men the name of Jesus, for it is the name of our salvation.

May it be to us and to all your people the name that is above every name, the name to be honoured, trusted, and adored, now and for evermore.

Frank Colquhoun

EPIPHANY

THE WISE MEN   **40**

Lord God, we remember how you led the wise men to Bethlehem by the light of a star. Guide us as we travel to the heavenly city that we and all men may know Jesus as the true and living way, for his name's sake.

M. H. Botting's collection

FOLLOWING THE STAR   **41**

God our Father, you gave to the wise men
the sign of the star,
understanding of how it pointed the way to Jesus and
determination to follow that way.
Give to us along the paths of our lives
guidance for the way you choose for us,
understanding of your word to us and
the will to trust and obey you,
till we come to your eternal glory.

(Matt. 2: 1–2, 9–10)   *J. C.*

EPIPHANY 1   The Baptism of Jesus

42   THE SERVICE OF MEN

Heavenly Father, who sent the Holy Spirit on your Son at his baptism to anoint him for the service of mankind: send your Spirit now to us who have been made your children by adoption and grace, that we may follow in his steps and work for the coming of his kingdom, to the glory of his name.

Frank Colquhoun

43   HIS BAPTISM AND OURS

Almighty Father, who spoke from heaven at the baptism of Jesus and declared him to be the Son you love, upon whom the Holy Spirit descended:

As Christ was raised from the dead through your glory, help us and all who are baptized into his death to live a new life as your children, in the power of the Holy Spirit.

(Luke 3: 22; Rom. 6: 4)   *J. C.*

EPIPHANY 2   The First Disciples

44   THE BEGINNINGS OF DISCIPLESHIP

May your Holy Spirit, Lord, continue to work graciously, patiently and effectively with those whose path to faith is hard, long, and surrounded by difficulties.

May he continue so to prepare the hearts of those who shall hear Jesus' sudden call 'Follow me' that they readily and willingly respond.

And may we and all the company of your people grow day by day in numbers, in experience, and in devotion to Jesus, our Saviour.

(Matt. 9: 9)   *J. C.*

THE FLOCK OF THE GREAT SHEPHERD 45

God of peace, whose Son our Lord Jesus was brought back
from the dead to become the great Shepherd of the sheep through
the blood of the eternal covenant: equip us with everything good
for doing your will, that our lives may always be pleasing to you
through Jesus Christ, to whom be glory for ever and ever.

(Heb. 13: 20–1) *Frank Colquhoun*

EPIPHANY 3 Signs of Glory

THE WEDDING AT CANA 46

Forgive us, Lord Jesus, because our faith is often not strong
enough, and because we hesitate to obey your commands when
we do not understand their intentions.

Then may ours be the obedient hands that find everyday
water transformed into the wine of lives that reflect your glory
among men.

(John 2: 1–11) *J. C.*

FEEDING THE FIVE THOUSAND 47

O Lord, who used the gift of one to fill the need of
thousands, help us so to care for others that without shame or
despair we may offer you all we have, to the glory of your name.

(John 6: 1–14) *Susan Williams*

EPIPHANY 4 The New Temple

THE CLEANSING OF THE TEMPLE 48

O Lord, who drove from the temple those whose aim it was
to make money, drive from our hearts the desire above all others
to own things and to do well in this life. May we, who are your
Church and Temple, be filled with you alone, so that we may
show your glory to the world and bring healing in your name.

(John 2: 13–16) *Susan Williams*

49 THE WOMAN AT THE WELL

Lord Jesus, Saviour of the world,
    we thank you for the record of how you
  set aside the conventions of the day
    that maintained barriers
      between Jew and Samaritan, man and woman;
  revealed yourself to the woman of Samaria; and
  offered her the living water.
Make yourself known in our sinful and divided world today.
Break down the barriers that separate us
    from each other, and from you.
Grant that many may find eternal satisfaction in you,
  the one who gives water that springs up
      to everlasting life, and
  the one by whom all men may worship the Father
      in Spirit and in truth.

(John 4: 4–14)

J. C.

EPIPHANY 5   The Wisdom of God

50 AROUSING THE NATION

O God of the nations, when corruption abounds
    and Christians grow cynical;
when racialism is rampant
    and Christians seek their own interests;
when consciences are stifled
    and it is safer to keep silent—
      then call out your prophets!
Give them courage to speak,
    clarity in doing so,
    and a burning constraint
        which will not let them be silent,
      by the power of your Holy Spirit.

J. Wheatley Price

AROUSING THE CHURCH 51

O God, rouse your church,
    lest we sleep and miss men's need of you
    and your yearning love for men.
O God, cleanse your church,
    and forgive our lack of zeal for your kingdom.
O God, set your church ablaze with the fire of your Spirit,
    that we may spend and be spent
        for your gospel,
        your will, and
        your glory, all our days.
    Through Jesus Christ, our Lord.

George Appleton

AROUSING OUR FACULTIES 52

Lord, we have found out so much knowledge and yet possess so little wisdom. We pray that in your mercy you will save us from ourselves. Help us to learn the right use of nature no less quickly than we unlock her new treasures; and give us hearts and wills made new in Christ to dedicate your gifts of knowledge to the service of others and to the praise of your name.

Timothy Dudley-Smith

EPIPHANY 6   Parables

SPREADING THE WORD 53

Give insight, Lord God, to those who translate the Bible.
May the Holy Spirit help them
    to understand the meaning of the original text,
    to recognize the force of the ideas which it expresses,
        and
    to interpret it accurately for those of a different culture.
May those to whom the Bible comes
  be enabled by the same Spirit
    to read it with understanding minds,
    to receive it with longing hearts, and
    to respond to it with ready wills,
        for love of Jesus as Lord and Saviour.

Michael Saward

54 SPREADING THE MESSAGE

Great God, author of good news,
>   warm the hearts of all who do the work of an evangelist;
>   open their mouths to proclaim the message of Christ;
>   and
>   grant that all who hear
>>   may turn from the bondage of sin,
>>   may seek the forgiveness of the Saviour, and
>>   may learn to obey him
>>>   whose service is perfect freedom,
>>>   and in whose name we pray.

Michael Saward

9TH SUNDAY BEFORE EASTER
(Septuagesima)   Christ the Teacher

55 PEACE THROUGH THE GOSPEL

We continue to pray O Lord for the peace of the world. Help us to see that there can be no peace among nations unless there is peace among men, and no peace among men until men have made their peace with you.

We claim the peace which comes from faith in Jesus Christ, that, having peace in our hearts, we may be at peace with our neighbours, and that peace between man and man may finally grow into peace between nation and nation.

We ask this in the name of the Prince of Peace, our Lord Jesus Christ.

(Eph. 2: 14–17)   *Simon H. Baynes*

56 THE SEED

Father, we thank you for the Bible, because rich and poor, wise and simple, old and young, sad and happy can find in it the answer to their needs. We pray that it will continue to be translated into the tongues men speak, so that all may know that you came to us in Christ; for his name's sake.

after Patricia Mitchell

8TH SUNDAY BEFORE EASTER
(Sexagesima)   Christ the Healer

HIS POWER AMONG HIS PEOPLE   57

Here in your house, O God, we pray for one another;
    give us each one the blessing we need.
We ask your healing for the sick,
    your strength for the tempted, and
    your joy for the downcast.
Answer the prayers which we try to put into words, and
    the prayers which you read in our hearts,
        according to your perfect love
        made known in Jesus Christ your Son our Lord.

Jamie Wallace

THANKSGIVING FOR HIS POWER TO HEAL   58

We give you our praise, Lord God,
    for your creation of our human bodies
        with their ability to resist and overcome
            so much infection and disease;
    for your power at work in Jesus Christ,
        who gave himself in the healing of the sick;
    for your love which constrains men and women today
        to care for the sick and to work for their healing;
    for your grace in hearing the prayer of faith
        when we bring before you those who are ill; and
    for every evidence you give us
        that your children can still be made whole
            through Jesus Christ,
        who is the same, yesterday, today, and for ever.

(Mark 1: 32-4; Heb. 13: 8)   *J. C.*

59   LOVE AND FAITH IN HIS PEOPLE

Heavenly Father, help us in our lives
        to reflect the love of your Son,
    who healed those who had need of healing and
    who has done everything well.
Help us also to have such faith in his power to heal
        that we are constrained
                to bring the needy to him and
                to ask for their healing
                        in prayer that is powerful and effective;
        for love of the sick, and to your glory.

(Luke 9: 11; Mark 7: 37 & 2: 5; James 5: 16)   *J. C.*

7TH SUNDAY BEFORE EASTER
(Quinquagesima)   Christ the Friend of Sinners

---

60   REPENTANCE AND A NEW LIFE

Lord God, we have loved those very sins
        which have been our downfall.
We repent, and declare to you
        our need of forgiveness, and
        our longing that we may bring you
                not only words of confession
                but lives that are renewed
                        by your healing of the wayward, and
                        by your compassion on the needy.
Truly the ways of the Lord are right;
        keep us walking in them by your grace.

(Hos. 14: 1–4, 14)   *J. C.*

61   COMFORT FOR THE CONTRITE

We worship you, Lord God,
        because you are high and holy,
        yet revive the spirit of the lowly
        and the heart of the contrite.

You have seen our ways, and yet you
      heal us,
      guide us, and
      restore comfort to us.
We love you and thank you, because
    even on our lips
      you create praise, and
    even to those who are far off
      you bring peace,
          through Jesus Christ, the Friend of sinners.

(Isa. 57: 15–19)   *J. C.*

FORGIVENESS AND NEW LIFE   **62**

Have mercy, gracious God, upon the world and upon us.
Forgive our sins and teach us, while there is yet time, to walk in
your way and turn to your light, as it shines in Jesus Christ, our
Saviour.   *Jamie Wallace*

OUR FEELINGS; CHRIST'S FORGIVENESS   **63**

Lord and Father, when our sins and failures overwhelm us,
and we feel far from your presence, show us the face of Christ, in
whom we are forgiven.   *Susan Williams*

ASH WEDNESDAY

PRESENT POWERLESSNESS; NEW LIFE PROMISED   **64**

Saviour, we thank you for showing us,
      in the perfection of your life,
    that by ourselves we can do nothing good or holy.
Since apart from you we can do nothing,
    we praise and thank you for the promise
      that in your love and power we can do all things.
Take our sin away;
Raise us with you to newness of life,
    so that our lives, taking all their goodness from you,
      may give you all the glory, for ever and ever.

(John 15: 5–7)   *Jamie Wallace*

6TH SUNDAY BEFORE EASTER
(Lent 1)   The King and the Kingdom: Temptation

65   A SAVIOUR TEMPTED LIKE US

We praise you, our heavenly Father, that you have given
your Son as a Saviour who was made so like us that he has been
tempted in every way and can sympathize with our weaknesses.

We offer you the thanks of our hearts that we can approach
your throne of grace with confidence because Jesus, our great
and sinless high priest, is seated with you in heaven.

With love and praise we acknowledge our dependence on
you alone, that we may receive mercy and may find grace to help
us in our time of need;
            through our Lord Jesus Christ.

(Heb. 2: 18; 4: 14–16)   *J.C.*

66   TEMPTATION IN MINISTRY

Lord, you sent us out into all the world to make followers
        from every nation.
Help us to resist the temptations which you yourself
        overcame;
keep us from offering to the hungry nothing but bread;
        from presenting proofs instead of a Person; and
        from serving the forces of this world in the hope that
                they will serve us, your messengers.
We ask it in the name of our victorious Saviour.

(Matt. 4: 1–10)   *Susan Williams*

67   VICTORY IN PERSONAL TEMPTATION

Teach us, O God, so to use this season of Lent
        that we may be drawn closer to our Lord,
and in fellowship with him may learn
        to hate sin,
        to overcome temptation, and
        to grow in holiness,
that our lives may be strengthened for your service
                and used for your glory.
We ask this in Christ's name.

                                    Frank Colquhoun

5TH SUNDAY BEFORE EASTER
(Lent 2)   The King and the Kingdom: Conflict

WEEPING OVER THE CITY   68

We confess Lord that we too often remain unmoved by that
which made our Master weep.

Help us to have a sense of the tragedy in men's ignorance of
the peace that can come to them through him.

Give us such an awareness of the love of Christ that we shall
be constrained to live as his ambassadors, making known to men
his message of reconciliation,

For the spread of his glory and the advance of his kingdom.

(Luke 19: 41–2; 2 Cor. 6: 19–20)   *J. C.*

THE TEMPTER   69

Lord of all might and majesty:
      Blind the power of Satan;
      Block the progress of Satan;
      Banish the presence of Satan,
            and free his prisoners,
through the holy name of Jesus.

                              Michael Saward

4TH SUNDAY BEFORE EASTER
(Lent 3)   The King and the Kingdom: Suffering

70   BEING WHAT WE PROFESS TO BE

Son of Man, our Saviour, we remember that your sternest judgements were reserved for the religious people of your day, because they failed to live up to their profession.

Forbid it, Lord, that we, who so often and so readily take your name upon our lips, should come under the same condemnation.

Help us in this season of Lent to search our hearts and examine our lives, and to have done with all hypocrisy and pretence.

May we be what we seem to be, putting our creed into practice, and bearing a witness before men that will be to your honour.

(Matt. 23: 1–33)   *Frank Colquhoun*

71   DENYING OURSELVES

Lord Christ, who for love of our souls
    chose the costliest following of the Father's will:
Forgive us for having so often
    followed the easy path of selfish desire;
set your law of sacrifice within our hearts;
    that we may be ready to deny ourselves
    and to walk courageously in your steps,
        our crucified Redeemer, who lives and reigns
        in the glory of the Father and the Holy Spirit,
    one God for evermore.

Adapted by Frank Colquhoun

CRUCIFIED WITH CHRIST 72

Help us Lord not to shrink from being crucified with Christ,
  so that we no longer live,
  yet Christ lives in us.
May we live day by day by faith in the Son of God,
  who loved us and gave himself for us,
  and by whose wounds we have been healed.

(Gal. 2: 20; 1 Pet. 2: 24)   J. C.

3RD SUNDAY BEFORE EASTER
(Lent 4)   The King and the Kingdom: Transfiguration

BEHOLDING HIS MAJESTY 73

God of Moses and Elijah, Father of Jesus Christ our Lord:
We recall that awesome moment on the mount
    when Peter, James, and John heard your voice
    and saw the touch of glory on your Son.
May we by faith behold his majesty
    and give him the obedience and reverence which are his due;
and to his name be dominion and power,
    now and for evermore.

(Matt. 17: 1–3)   *Roger Pickering*

OUR EYES FIXED ON JESUS 74 X

Give to us Lord the ability and the desire through all the anxieties and pleasures of daily life to fix our eyes on Jesus, from whom our faith derives and in whom it will be brought to completion.

May our gaze so rest upon his glory that earthly things cease to assume an importance greater than is really theirs;

and may we have faith in such a measure that we shall be able to minister to others in his power and in his name.

(Heb. 12: 2; Luke 9: 32; Matt. 17: 19, 20)   J. C.

75 THE MOUNTAIN TOP

Teach us Lord Jesus that in our lives we need hours and days to behold your glory.

Help us to take time to meet you, and to learn from you, and then return renewed to serve you, your church, and the world for which you gave yourself.

J. C.

2ND SUNDAY BEFORE EASTER
(Lent 5) (Passion Sunday)   The King and the Kingdom: Victory

76 THE GRAIN OF WHEAT

Lord God, teach us more of the meaning of our Saviour's words when he spoke of the ear of wheat falling to the ground and dying, that it might produce many seeds.

May we die to sin, that we may be set free to live a new life. May we die with Christ, that we may live with him as your servants in eternal life, by your grace.

(John 12: 24–6; Rom. 6: 2–12, 22)   *J. C.*

77 CHRIST'S VICTORY IN OUR LIVES

O God, the Father of all mankind,
        who loved the world so much
        that you gave your only Son to die for man's salvation:
make us, who have been redeemed by his precious blood,
        to die with him to sin,
        to rise with him to righteousness, and
        to walk with him in newness of life;
through the merits of the same Jesus Christ our Lord.

(I Pet. 2: 24)   *Frank Colquhoun*

THE CROSS OF CHRIST   78

Loving Lord Jesus,
    when you took up your cross for our sakes
        and carried it to Golgotha,
    you did it in the sight of the multitudes,
        and yet alone.
Help us to be ready to deny ourselves and to carry our cross
    as those crucified with you,
        but never alone,
        for you live in us.
In the darkest hours
    reassure us that the life we live in the body
    we live by faith in you, the Son of God;
        for you loved us and gave yourself for us,
           who praise your holy name.

(John 19: 17; Matt. 17: 24; Gal. 2: 20)   *J. C.*

PALM SUNDAY
(Lent 6)   **The Way of the Cross**

CONFRONTING THE ENEMY   79

O Lord, who rode straight into the power of the enemy
    to suffer and to die:
give us both the strength to follow you
        to the centres of opposition in this world, and
    the confidence which confronts the power of evil
        with your love.

(Matt. 21: 1–14, 16: 21)   *Susan Williams*

80   ACCLAMATION OF JESUS CHRIST

Lord Jesus Christ,
    as you entered the rebellious city of Jerusalem,
    so enter our sinful hearts
    and make us wholly subject to you.
As your disciples welcomed your coming,
    so make us ready to lay at your feet
    all we have and are.
May we not only confess and worship you on earth,
    but also be among that great multitude who in heaven
        shall wear white robes,
        shall have palm branches in their hands, and
        shall cry 'Salvation belongs to our God,
            who sits on the throne,
            and to the Lamb'.

(Luke 19: 28–44; Rev. 7: 9–10)   *Adapted from the Book of Common Order*

81   A FULLER UNDERSTANDING

Keep us, Lord, from being so earthbound
    that we fail to recognize the spiritual significance
    of what happens before our very eyes.
Keep us from having so limited a view of Jesus of Nazareth
    that we fail to respond to him as Jesus Christ,
        who loved us, and gave himself for our sins—
        and not for ours only,
        but also for the sins of the whole world.

(Luke 19: 42; Matt. 21: 11; 1 John 2: 2)   *J. C.*

HOLY WEEK: MONDAY

THE DISCIPLES WITH THEIR MASTER   82

Lord Christ, we recall at this time how on that solemn passover night you met with your disciples in the upper room and hallowed bread and wine as the memorials of your body and blood.

We thank you for this sacrament of our redemption and for all that it reveals to us of your love; and we pray that whenever we meet at your table to obey your command 'Do this in remembrance of me' we may know your risen presence in our midst and feed upon you, the true Bread from heaven, till we come to your everlasting kingdom.

(Luke 22: 12–19; I Cor. 11: 23–6)   *Frank Colquhoun*

A DEEPER DISCIPLESHIP   83

Heavenly Father, as we remember
    that first Holy Week in Jerusalem,
  give us a renewed vision of your Son, our Saviour.
May our commitment to him be firmer.
May our love for him be greater.
May our obedience to him be more loyal.
May our sharing of his eucharist be more thankful.
May our concern for all for whom he died be more real.
May our lives be more worthy of him, our Lord Jesus Christ.

J. C.

HOLY WEEK: TUESDAY

84   STRENGTH IN TEMPTATION

O God of all power and love:
As you sent your angel to strengthen our Lord
     in his temptation and agony;
So strengthen now all who are in temptation,
                    all who are in agony, and
                    all the dying.
Give them victory and peace,
     through him who overcame, Jesus Christ our Lord.

(Luke 22: 43)   *George Appleton*

85   FRIGHTENED DISCIPLES

You know us, God, and you know our weaknesses.
Have mercy on us and on all Christian people when we are
tempted to cast away our confidence in Christ.
When the high and mighty are against him, and when the
crowd cries for blood, help us to cling to his cross and to behold
his face.
As you saved and delivered the first disciples so, by the
power of the resurrection, save and deliver us too, we pray,
through the same Jesus Christ our Lord.

                                                    Dick Williams

HOLY WEEK: WEDNESDAY

THE HIGH PRIEST **86**

Have mercy, O Lord,
  on all who bear high office and abuse its authority;
  all who plot courses of political action
    for the sole purpose of protecting their own positions;
  all who persecute prophets because of the evil they expose;
  all who manufacture a lie for public consumption;
  all who treat prophets and public alike as pawns and puppets;
  on all such, everywhere, O Lord have mercy.
Help them to worship truth, and to give God the glory.
Teach them to know and to understand,
        to believe and to trust,
          that for the mighty as for the meek
            it is only by losing our life that we find it,
            only by dying that we live,
            only by following Christ that we lead men;
              for his name's sake.

Dick Williams

PILATE **87**

Have mercy, O Lord,
  on all who are called to the terrible loneliness
    of giving judgement;
  all who know that upon their conclusions
    rest the lives of others;
  all who are the object of bribery or menace.
Give them great courage and great goodness.
Make them wise in heart,
        humble in spirit,
        accurate in thought,
        brave in decision,
        resolute in life.
Make them righteous and give them peace,
        through Jesus Christ our Lord.

Dick Williams

MAUNDY THURSDAY The Lord's Supper

88 WASHING THE DISCIPLES' FEET

Son of Man, who on the night before your passion took towel and water and washed the feet of your disciples: give us understanding of what you have done, and teach us to follow the example of your humility, that by love we may serve one another for love of you, our Saviour and Lord.

(John 13: 1–17) *Frank Colquhoun*

89 PARDON AND NEW LIFE

Dear Lord Jesus, at this evening hour,
      as we come to your table to receive the broken bread,
      help us to know
            that your body was truly broken
                  for the sins of each one of us, and
            that in you we have pardon for all that is past.
As we share in the cup of the new covenant,
      help us to know
            that your blood was truly shed for our
                  redemption, and
            that in you we have new life for evermore.
Lord Jesus,
      yours is the love and obedience we bring this evening,
      and yours is the power and the glory for evermore.

J. C.

90 'IN REMEMBRANCE, . . . UNTIL HE COMES'

Lord Jesus,
      as we have come together
            around your table in this solemn hour:
Help us to look back
      with more loving remembrance
            of you and the price you have paid for us,
      with deeper thankfulness for our redemption, and
      with greater understanding
            of the new covenant in your blood.
Help us also to look forward
      as we eat this bread and drink this cup,
      proclaiming your death until you come again
      in that glory that is yet to be revealed.

(1 Cor. 11: 24–6) *J. C.*

GOOD FRIDAY   The Death of Christ

MEDITATION BEFORE THE CROSS   91

Holy and mighty Father,
    you gave your only Son to be a sacrifice for us—
        for us, who all like sheep have gone astray,
        for us, who every one has turned to his own way,
        for us, whose iniquity you have laid on him.
In your mercy look on us
    as we meditate and pray before his cross.
Give us faith so to comprehend the mystery of his passion
    that we enter into the fellowship of his sufferings.
Let his wounds be our healing,
    his cross our redemption, and
    his death our life;
        through all that makes him 'Jesus Christ, our Lord'.

(Isa. 53: 6; Phil. 3: 10)   *Anon.*

'BY HIS WOUNDS WE ARE HEALED'   92

Almighty and loving God,
    we confess that it is all too true
    that we, like sheep, have gone astray
    and that each of us has turned to his own way.
We abhor ourselves when we are reminded
    that our Lord was despised and rejected
        by the men for whose transgressions he was pierced.
It is with all humility that we take for ourselves
    the healing we have by his wounds and
    the peace that has been brought us
        by the punishment which was upon him.
We offer ourselves now to him so that
    the will of the Lord may be prospered,
        and after the suffering of his soul
    he may see the light of life and be satisfied
as he hears the resolve of those he has justified
    to live the new life to the glory of his name.

(Isa. 53: 3–11)   *J. C.*

93   IN DEBT TO CHRIST

Lord Jesus, we praise you for your redeeming love
    and for all that you have done for us.
As we bow in penitence before the cross
    we gratefully acknowledge the debt we owe,
    for ours was the sin you bore,
        ours the ransom you paid, and
        ours the salvation you won.
Lord Jesus, accept our thanksgiving
    and make us more worthy of your love,
    for your love's sake.

Frank Colquhoun

94   FULL ASSURANCE OF FAITH

Our Saviour Jesus, in silent, humble and thankful worship
    we thank you for your blood shed for us;
    we thank you for the confidence you give us
        to enter the Most Holy Place;
    we thank you for the new and living way opened for us;
    we worship you as our own great priest
        over the house of God;
    we love you as the one who has sprinkled our hearts
        and cleansed our guilt.
So at this time of worship together
    we draw near to the Father himself with a sincere heart.
We pray that we may be given the full assurance of faith
    and may go out from here
        holding unswervingly to the hope we profess and
        encouraged as the Day approaches
            when you will be revealed in your great glory.

(Heb. 10: 19–25; 2 Thess. 1: 10)   *J. C.*

THE DYING THIEF **95**

Lord Jesus, King of glory, we praise you for the faith
 that is not of ourselves, but is the gift of God.
We praise you that at the very hour
 when by every human standard
  it seemed beyond all reason
 the dying thief
  proclaimed you as Lord and King,
  confessed his own sin and guilt, and
  received your promise for eternity.
Give this same faith now
 to those at the end of a life spent far from you,
 to those who have abandoned all hope,
 to those in the hour of death.
As in love we commit them all to you
 we ask that we ourselves may be kept
  in the faith that God can do
   immeasurably more than all we ask or imagine.
To him be glory in the church and in Christ Jesus,
 now in our generation
 and for ever and ever!

(Luke 23: 40–3; Eph. 2: 8 & 3: 20–1)   *J. C.*

EASTER EVE

JOSEPH OF ARIMATHEA **96**

Bless, O Lord,
 all who worship you in secret;
 all in whose hearts is growing an undeclared allegiance;
 all whose life is laden with a treasure they need to pour
  out at your feet;
 all who know with greater certainty each day
  that they have found the pearl of greatest price.
Then by the power of the cross, O Christ,
 claim your victory in their hearts,
 and lead them to the liberty of being seen by all men
  to be yours and
  to be lovers of your dear name.

Dick Williams

EASTER DAY   The Resurrection of Christ

97   EASTER WORD AND SACRAMENT

Living Lord, vanquisher of sin and death,
    come among us in your risen power
and make your presence known to us
    in word and sacrament this Easter day.
Speak your message of peace to our hearts;
    show us your wounded hands and side; and
    send us forth to your service
        in the power of the Holy Spirit, and
        to the glory of your name.

(John 20: 19–23)   *Frank Colquhoun*

98   THE SONG OF EVERY CREATURE

God of our salvation, we rejoice in you this Easter Day
    and share in the praise of heaven and earth
    as we declare:
        'To him who sits on the throne
            and to the Lamb
        be praise
            and honour
            and glory
            and power
        for ever and ever!'

(Rev. 5: 13)   *J. C.*

99   RESURRECTION LIFE IN HIS DISCIPLES

Lord Jesus, we thank you that you showed
        your resurrection triumph and glory
    in speaking by name to lonely, weeping Mary,
    in bringing the word of peace to the fearful disciples,
    in walking and talking
        with downcast Cleopas and his companion.
Give the same joy of your presence today
        to those who are alone and
        to your whole church,

that we shall all look forward in joyful confidence
    to being with you in your heavenly glory.

(John 20: 10–19; Luke 24: 13–32)   *J. C.*

EASTER HOPE   100

We worship you, our living, conquering Lord,
    because by your death you have broken the power of
        death
    and by your glorious resurrection you have brought life
        and immortality to light.
As those who partake of your victory
    we pray that we may continually rejoice in this hope,
    and live on earth as those whose citizenship
        is in heaven, where you reign
        in the glory of the Father and the Holy Spirit
            for ever and ever.

(Heb. 2: 14; 2 Tim. 1: 10; Phil. 3: 20)   *Frank Colquhoun*

THE IMPULSE TO MISSION   101

Lord Jesus, set our hearts on fire with your love that, with
joy and thankfulness in our hearts, we, your followers, may once
again be sent out inspired by the message of the cross and by the
joy of Easter.

Joyce Francis

102 THE EASTER GOSPEL FOR ALL THE NATIONS

God, who gave Jesus Christ to be born among men
    that he might be the Saviour of the world:
We join in praising you
    that you raised him from the dead;
    that you enable us to confess with our mouths 'Jesus is
       Lord' and
    that we and all who call on this name will be saved.
Fill us with such love for you
    that your church will be impelled
        to make the name of Jesus known to those who do
        not call upon him.
Enable us by our obedience
    to roll back the reproach to your holy name
    that results from our silence;
        for the sake of him who richly blesses all who call
        on him,
            Jesus our Lord.

(1 John 5: 14; Rom. 10: 8–15)   *J. C.*

EASTER WEEK

103 FAITH, HOPE, AND LOVE

Lord, at this Easter time we ask you to increase our faith,
    our hope and our love.
Give us the faith that overcomes the world and enables us to
    face both life and death calm and unafraid.
Give us the hope that looks beyond this mortal life and grasps
    hold of the things unseen and eternal.
Give us the love that binds us more closely to one another
    and to you, our risen Lord;
    to whom be all glory and praise,
    dominion and power, now and for ever.

(Luke 17: 5; Rom. 15: 13; 1 Thess. 3: 12)   *Frank Colquhoun*

THE RISEN CHRIST'S CONTINUING PRESENCE   104

Lord Jesus, our risen Saviour,
>we rejoice in your mighty victory
>>over sin and death.
You are the Prince of life;
>you are alive for evermore.
Help us to know your presence,
>not only as we worship you here,
>>but at home,
>>at work, and
>>wherever we go;
>>>for your great name's sake.

Michael Botting

EASTER 1   The Upper Room

PEACE BE WITH YOU   105

As Christians, we ought not to fear, and yet we are afraid—of the neighbours, of the people we work with, and even of our own families. Our faith is often to be found only behind the closed doors of our own hearts.

Yet, O Lord, you come to us with peace, and your coming is enough to fill our hearts with joy.

Burst the bonds of the fear that keeps us silent, and send us out, with your message not only in our hearts but on our lips, to the praise of your name.

(John 20: 19–21)   *Ian D. Bunting*

THOMAS   106

Our Lord and God, forgive the doubting heart in each of us which questions your resurrection. We are men and women of our age, and want to see and touch before we believe. And yet we thank you for that blessing, reserved for those who do not see and yet believe.

Grant us that faith which looks to Jesus, risen from the dead, our Saviour and our living Lord.

(John 20: 24–9)   *Ian D. Bunting*

107   THE BREAD OF LIFE

Forgive us, Lord Jesus, for so often being content with the
second-best in our spiritual lives.
Thank you that you are the bread of life, and for your promise
that he who comes to you will never go hungry.
From now on, give us this bread, and help us day by day to
feed on you, and so to live for ever.

(John 6: 34, 35, 57, 58)   *J. C.*

EASTER 2   **The Emmaus Road**

108   THE COMPANION OF OUR PILGRIMAGE

Risen Lord, who on the first Easter day drew near to your
two disciples on the Emmaus road, and at evening stayed with
them in their village home: be our unseen companion along the
daily journey of our life, and at the ending of the day come and
abide with us in our dwellings; for your love's sake.

(Luke 24: 13–35)   *Frank Colquhoun*

109   WHEN WE ARE DOWNCAST

Lord, we do not always find it easy to recognize you when
you come to us. Our spirits are often downcast because we have
created our own image of what we expect from you and then fail
to perceive you as you really are.

Reveal yourself to us. Open our eyes to undiscovered
treasures of your word. Meet us in the breaking of bread. Set our
hearts on fire with love for you, and send us on our way rejoicing
in your presence as our living Lord.

(Luke 24: 13–35)   *Ian D. Bunting*

The Good Shepherd

HIS SHEEP 110

Lord Jesus Christ,
   Good Shepherd who gave your life for the sheep:
   Gather into your fold those who have wandered away,
   feed those who are hungry,
   give rest in green pastures to those who are weary of life,
   bind up the wounds of those who are injured,
   strengthen those who are weak, and
   guide us all in right pathways,
      for your name's sake.

(John 10: 11)   *David Silk*

THE GOOD SHEPHERD AND HIS FLOCK 111

Lord Jesus, whom we love as our good Shepherd:
   We thank you that you laid down your life
               for your sheep,
      and pray that we may care more
               for others of your flock.
   We trust you because you know your sheep,
      and pray that we may grow to know you more.
   We praise you for your voice that your sheep can hear,
      and pray that we may learn
               to be more ready to obey it.
   We rejoice that you have come that we may have life,
      and pray that we may live more
               as those who have it to the full.
   We acknowledge that you alone
               are the gate for the sheep,
      and pray that we may know more
         from daily experience with you
      that we can find no other entry
         to the blessings of your green pastures.

(John 10: 1–18)   *J. C.*

112   A MODERN PRAYER IN THE CELTIC TRADITION

Good Shepherd,
> be over me to shelter me,
> under me to uphold me,
> behind me to direct me,
> before me to lead me,
> about me to protect me,
> ever with me to save me,
> above me to lift me,
and bring me to the green pasture of eternal life.

David Adam

EASTER 3   The Lakeside

---

113   THE PRESENCE OF THE RISEN LORD

Remind us Father that our daily lives will be wearisome and fruitless unless the risen power and presence of the Lord Jesus transforms us. Grant that in the week ahead we may know his presence with us in all we do, and may be ready to hear and to obey his voice as he calls us to follow him.

J. C.

114   UNDESERVED BLESSINGS OF CHRIST'S PRESENCE

Lord Jesus, when we are tempted
> to abandon some great enterprise
> > to which you have called us,
> draw near to encourage us,
> > as you drew near to the disciples
> > > when they had gone back
> > > > to their life as fishermen.
When we imagine our labours pointless,
> give us your command,
> > as you commanded the disciples to cast their net.
When we are tired but still have more toil before us,
> provide for us in our need,
> > as you provided for the disciples
> > > with that lighted fire on shore

When we are about the daily occupations of life,
    bless us with your presence,
        as you did when you were present
            with the disciples at breakfast.
When we just don't deserve your blessing,
    come to us in our faithlessness,
        as you came to the faithless disciples,
            bringing the calm and joy of your presence.

(John 21: 1–12)   *J. C.*

The Resurrection and the Life

NEW LIFE FOR THE CHURCH   **115**

Lord Jesus,
    when we are imprisoned and useless,
        take away the gravestone and let us out;
    when we are powerless and stagnant,
        strip off the graveclothes and let us go;
    when we are ineffective and joyless,
        remove whatever gags us and let us speak.
Then, by your grace, may many put their faith in you,
        Jesus the Saviour.

(John 11: 38–44; 12: 9–11)   *J. C.*

JESUS, THE COMFORT OF THE SORROWING   **116**

O God our Father, we pray for those whose life is saddened
by the death of a relative or a friend. Be with them in their
loneliness. Give them faith to lift their eyes beyond their present
trouble and to fasten them on Jesus, the one who died and rose
again, and who lives for evermore.

M. H. Botting's collection

EASTER 4   **The Charge to Peter**

117   THE PASTORAL MINISTRY

Pour out your Holy Spirit, O Lord,
on all whom you have called to serve your Church
as pastors and teachers.
Give them wise and understanding hearts;
fill them with a true love for your people;
make them holy and keep them humble;
that they may be faithful shepherds
and feed the flock committed to their care,
ever seeking your glory
and the increase of your kingdom;
through Jesus Christ our Lord.

(Acts. 20: 28; 1 Pet. 5: 2–3)   *Frank Colquhoun*

118   FEEDING CHRIST'S SHEEP

Merciful father, lover of souls and redeemer of mankind,
may your church show your compassion on all who do not know
you as you are revealed in your Son Jesus Christ.

Let your gospel be preached with grace and power to those
who have not known it; turn the hearts of those who resist it; and
bring home to your fold those who have gone astray; that there
may be one flock under one shepherd, Jesus Christ our Lord.

(John 10: 16)   *Episcopal Church, USA*

119   THE WAY, THE TRUTH, AND THE LIFE

Great God, source of all truth and Lord of all life, it was your
Son Jesus Christ who taught us to call you 'Father' and to
acknowledge that none can come to you except through him.

Encourage us to love and care for those who search for you
under other names, and to rejoice in qualities in them which
come from you.

Keep us from ever denying Christ as the only mediator
between you and mankind, and fire us with the desire to make
him known as the only Saviour and Lord, who is Emmanuel,
God among us:

in whose name we pray.

(Matt. 1: 23; John 14: 6; 1 Tim. 2: 5)   *Michael Saward*

EASTER 5 Going to the Father

THE SPIRIT AS GUIDE 120

Holy Spirit, who speaks to us:
    teach us to recognize your voice,
    incline us to follow your guiding,
    help us more fully to know Jesus, our Saviour.

(John 16: 13–15) *J. C.*

THE SPIRIT OF TRUTH 121

O Holy Spirit of God, inspirer of all that is good and
beautiful and true in life, come into our hearts this day and fill us
with your light and strength. Help us to hate all sin and
selfishness, and to fight against them with unfaltering courage
and resolve. And because we are weak, and cannot prevail
without your help, strengthen us and give us the victory for
Christ's sake.

Harold E. Evans

ASCENSIONTIDE The Ascension of Christ

THE EXALTED LORD OF OUR LIVES 122

Almighty and everlasting God, we worship and adore you
because you have exalted your Son our Lord Jesus Christ and
caused him to triumph mightily.
    We serve him as King of glory, enthroned at your right
        hand.
    We trust him as our great High Priest, who has entered
        the heavenly sanctuary to intercede for us.
    We obey him as Lord of the church, to whom all
        authority has been given.
    To him who sits upon the throne and to the Lamb be
praise and honour, glory and dominion, for ever and ever.

(Phil. 2: 9; Heb. 12: 2 & 6: 19–20; Eph. 5: 23–4; Rev. 7: 9–12)
Frank Colquhoun

123   '. . . TO PREPARE A PLACE FOR US'

We praise you, God our Father, that our ascended Lord has entered heaven as the forerunner of his people and has gone to prepare a place for us, so that where he is, there we may be also.

May our faith that he now reigns at your right hand make heaven a more real and wonderful place to us; and may we be enabled to lay hold more firmly on the hope that is set before us, that we may come at last where he has gone before, through the merits and mediation of his great name.

(John 14: 2–3; Rev. 11: 15; 1 Pet. 3: 22; Heb. 6: 18)   *Frank Colquhoun*

124   'CROWNED WITH GLORY NOW'

Almighty God and Father, we thank you
    that the head that once was crowned with thorns
        is crowned with glory now.
We celebrate with joy the kingship of Jesus.
Give us grace to acknowledge his rule
    in our lives as well as with our lips,
  and to serve his worldwide kingdom,
    that the day may be hastened
      when all nations shall own him Lord
      and he shall reign for ever and ever.

Frank Colquhoun

PENTECOST (Whitsunday)   The Gift of the Spirit

125   THE SPIRIT RENEWING THE CHURCH

Your Spirit, O God, came to the disciples through Jesus Christ our Lord: bless your disciples today with the same gift from the same Master, that they may find fullness of life in him, and serve him with joy and power all the days of their life, for his truth and mercy's sake.

Dick Williams

THE SPIRIT TEACHING THE CHURCH   126

Holy Spirit of God, on the day of Pentecost
        you came once for all to the church
        as the gift of the exalted Lord.
Come to us in your grace and power today,
        to make Jesus real to us,
        to teach us more about him, and
        to deepen our faith in him;
    that we may be changed into his likeness
        and be his witnesses in the world,
            to the glory of God the Father.

Frank Colquhoun

THE SPIRIT EMPOWERING THE CHURCH   127

We praise you, O God, because you gave the Holy Spirit to
the first Christians. You made Jesus real to them; you taught
them the truth and gave them power to witness boldly.

Fill us with the same Spirit, that we may know their
experience and follow their example; for Jesus' sake.

M. H. Botting's collection

THE SPIRIT UNITING THE CHURCH   128

Bless us Lord when we are all together in one place, and
grant that in our common life we may know the coming of your
Spirit.

May your fire come to rest on each of us, and then make us,
separately and together, preachers of your good news whom all
the world shall hear and understand;
                through Jesus Christ our Lord.

Dick Williams

PENTECOST 1 (Trinity Sunday) The Holy Trinity

129 TRINITARIAN FAITH

Eternal God, you have revealed yourself to us in your grace
    as Father, Son and Holy Spirit, the God of our salvation.
Help us firmly to believe in you,
        boldly to confess your name, and
        joyfully to worship you,
    one holy, glorious and undivided Trinity, for ever and ever.

Frank Colquhoun

130 EVERYDAY EXPERIENCE

The sacred Three be over me
    with my working hands this day,
    with the people on my way,
    with the labour and the toil,
    with the land and with the soil,
    with the tools that I take,
    with the things that I make,
    with the thoughts of my mind,
    with the sharing of mankind,
    with the love of my heart,
    with each one who plays a part.
The sacred Three be over me,
    the blessing of the Trinity.

David Adam

131 OUR LOVE AND OBEDIENCE

We praise you, God,
    for your Son, sent into the world to redeem us.
We praise you, God,
    for your Spirit, sent into our hearts to renew us.
We thank you, God,
    that you enable the redeemed to have the full rights
        of your children.
We thank you, God,
    that you enable the renewed to call you 'Abba, Father'.
As children of the King, we offer our love.

As heirs of the kingdom, we offer our obedience
to Father, Son and Holy Spirit,
three Persons and one God.

(Gal. 4: 4–7)   *J. C.*

PENTECOST 2 (Trinity 1)   The People of God

IMPLICATIONS OF BEING A REDEEMED PEOPLE   132

Lord of the Church,
enable your people to *be* the Church,
a redeemed people
a holy people
a united people
a missionary people
and in all things
a people gladly submissive to the truth
as it is found in Jesus.
In whose name we pray.

Michael Saward

A CONFESSION FOR THE CHURCH   133

O God, whose will it is that all your children should be one
in Christ, we pray for the unity of your church.
Pardon all our pride and our lack of faith, of understanding
and of charity, which are the cause of our divisions.
Deliver us from our narrow-mindedness, from our bitterness, from our prejudices.
Save us from considering as normal that which is a scandal
to the world and an offence to your love.
Teach us to recognize the gifts of your grace among all those
who call upon you and confess the faith of Jesus Christ our Lord.

Liturgy of the Reformed Church of France

The Church's Unity and Fellowship

134   JESUS SEEN IN THE CHURCH

We need your continuing grace, Lord Jesus,
    to live in harmony with one another,
    to be compassionate for others,
    to be humble before them,
    to be ready at any time to give the reason for our hope.
Help us to live such a continuing and effective witness
      to you as Lord
    that others may turn to you
    and may find all they need in you,
      their Lord and ours.

(1 Pet. 3: 8, 15)   *J. C.*

135   BAPTISM IN CHRIST AND THE GIFT OF THE SPIRIT

We praise you, heavenly Father, for your call and your promise to us and our children, and to all who are far off.

We thank you for grace to repent and for baptism in the name of Jesus Christ that our sins may be forgiven.

We adore you, the giver of the Holy Spirit, by whom we pray that we and your whole church may have power to live to the glory of three Persons and one God, eternal in power and majesty.

(Acts 2: 38–9)   *J. C.*

PENTECOST 3 (Trinity 2)   The Life of the Baptized

136   BLESSING AND WITNESS

O heavenly and eternal Father, pour your blessing upon all who are baptized in the name of three Persons and one God, in this country and in all lands. May we all grasp your majesty and might; may we be filled with your Holy Spirit, that the church today, like the early church, may preach and live the gospel of Christ in eagerness, power and love.

Grant this, O Lord, that your name may be honoured before the world.

Anon.

The Church's Confidence in Christ

TRUSTING AND OBEYING 137

Lord Jesus, we thank you that you ascended as King of heaven and earth and that you are in control of all things.

Help us to trust you when life is difficult and obey you at all times.

We ask this for the honour of your name.

M. H. Botting's collection

PENTECOST 4 (Trinity 3)
The Freedom of the Sons of God

LIVING AS HEIRS 138

We praise you our Father for all the privileges of being your sons through faith in Christ Jesus.

Help us to know the freedom of being united with him in baptism and clothed with him, and so to know his Spirit in our hearts that we may no longer live as slaves and prisoners of sin, but as heirs of your eternal kingdom;

by the merits of him whom you sent as our Redeemer.

(Gal. 3: 26 to 4: 7) *J.C.*

The Church's Ministry to the Individual

BEING BOLD TO SPEAK 139

Father, give us, each one, the wit and the will
at the right moment
to tell the truth we grasp
and speak of the Lord we love
to people we know
and strangers we meet;
for your glory's sake.

Jamie Wallace

140   THE EVANGELIST

Make us ready Lord, like Philip,
     to obey you when you call us to serve you,
     to hear you when you speak to guide us, and
     to tell the good news about Jesus
          to those who need him,
               that they may go on their way rejoicing.

(Acts 8: 26–38)   *J. C.*

PENTECOST 5 (Trinity 4)   The New Law

---

141   LIVING AS CHILDREN OF LIGHT

Help us Lord to realize how impossible it is for us relying only on our own efforts to attain your standards.

Inspire us Lord to give the love of our hearts more fully to you, with whom all things are possible.

Train us Lord to live as children of light, daily pleasing you by your indwelling Spirit;
     through our Saviour Jesus Christ.

(Matt. 19: 26; Eph. 5: 8, 10)   *J. C.*

The Church's Ministry to all Men

---

142   BECOMING WHAT WE OUGHT TO BE

Forgive us, Lord God our Father,
          that your holy church throughout all the world
     proclaims you so unconvincingly and
     serves you so half-heartedly.
Bless richly the people, the congregations and the orders
          that shame the rest of us
     by the way they live out the life of Christ
     and demonstrate the power the Holy Spirit gives.

Pour out the Holy Spirit
    to make the rest of your church
    like the best of your church—
        something able to turn the world upside down,
        something fit to be called the body of Christ.
We ask it for his sake.

Jamie Wallace

MEN BROUGHT TOGETHER AGAIN 143

Father, you have given all peoples one common origin,
    and your will is to gather them as one family in yourself.
Fill the hearts of all men
        with the fire of your love
        and the desire to ensure justice for
            all their brothers and sisters.
By sharing the good things you gave us, may we secure
        justice and equality for every human being,
        an end to all division, and
        a human society built on love and peace.

(Eph. 3: 15)   *From the Roman Missal*

PENTECOST 6 (Trinity 5)   The New Man

THE LOST SON 144

Together we give our thanks to you, our heavenly Father,
    for your compassion for all who are still a long way from
        you,
    for your embrace for all who confess themselves sinners
        unworthy to be called your children, and
    for your rich provision for all who return to you and find
        new life;
and we ask that you will bring us to joy for evermore
    in your house with all the redeemed
        through our Saviour Jesus Christ.

(Luke 15: 11–24)   *J. C.*

145 BARTIMAEUS

We intercede with you, almighty God,
   for all who are in darkness of soul.
Help them to turn to Jesus as truly Christ and Saviour;
   to be assured that he cares for them and knows them;
   to voice to him their dependence on his mercy;
   to trust him enough to ask great things of him; and
   to be ready to let go of all that would hinder them,
     or dishonour him,
   as they follow him along the way,
     praising your holy name.

(Mark 10: 46–52; Luke 18: 43)   *J. C.*

PENTECOST 7 (Trinity 6)   **The More Excellent Way**

---

146 LOVE

Almighty God, you have taught us in your word
  that the fruit of the Spirit is love.
Give us by your Spirit the realization of that love in our
  hearts:
   the love that is patient, kind, and envious of no one;
   the love that is never boastful, proud or rude;
   the love that is not self-seeking, nor easily angered;
   the love that keeps no record of wrongs
     nor delights in evil;
   the love that rejoices in the truth, and never fails.
Above all else help us, O God our Father,
  to know that Christ is love in person, and
   love is Christ in our hearts.

(1 Cor. 13; Gal. 5: 22)   *Llewellyn Cumings*

147 THE GREAT COMMANDMENTS

  We ask Lord that you will teach us day by day that your
people should love you with all their hearts, with all their souls,
with all their minds, and with all their strength, and should love
their neighbours as themselves.
  Help us today as we go out from this place so to live under
the guidance and power of your Spirit that we are not far from the
kingdom of God, and are worthy witnesses to the grace of our
Saviour Jesus Christ, in whose name we pray.

(Mark 12: 28–34)   *J. C.*

PENTECOST 8 (Trinity 7)   The Fruit of the Spirit

BEARING THE FRUIT OF THE SPIRIT   **148**

Heavenly Father, as your children we need to ask great
   things from you:
     let us show love to the unloveable;
     let us have that joy which no man can take from us;
     let us know peace where we could be worrying;
     let us have the patience that knows you are in control;
     let us exercise kindness
         when it would be easier to pass by;
     let us be marked by the goodness
         that does not relish evil;
     let us have the faithfulness that identifies us as Christ's;
     let us display the gentleness
         that seeks to gain no advantage;
     let us be guided by the self-control
         that seeks others' good.
Help us to keep our sinful nature,
     its passions and desires,
        crucified with Christ, our Lord and Saviour.

(Gal. 5: 22–4)   *J. C.*

THE LOVE THAT OVERCOMES   **149**

Lord Jesus, killed by hate and raised by love,
   help us to be your witnesses in a hostile world;
     to show most love where there is most hate, and
     to live united to one another until you come again.

Susan Williams

PENTECOST 9 (Trinity 8)　　　The Armour of God

150

STANDING OUR GROUND

We give you thanks, our Father,
　　that as you sent your Son Jesus into the world,
　　　　so he has sent us,
　　　　　　has given us his word, and
　　　　　　prays that you will protect us from the evil one.
May we have your gift of sure confidence
　　in all he has done for us;
So that we may be enabled in the face of all evil
　　to stand our ground,
　　　　and after we have done everything
　　　　　　to be found still standing;
　　　　　　　　Through the full armour of God, and
　　　　　　　　　through the grace by which it is given to us.

(John 17: 14–18; Eph. 6: 13)　　　　　　　　　　　　　　　*J. C.*

151

THOSE UNDER PRESSURE

Lord God, we pray for those in your church
　　who are finding it especially hard
　　　　to resist the assaults
　　　　　　that come upon them for Christ's sake, and
　　　　to bear witness to you before the hostile.
We ask that you will enable them to overcome
　　　　all temptation to think
　　　　　　that the forces ranged against them are merely human,
　　　　　　and
　　　　that they can therefore triumph
　　　　　　by their own resolution and skill alone.
Help them to remember that the struggle is
　　against unseen powers of this dark world, and
　　against spiritual forces of evil in the heavenly realms.
Show them how they need
　　your provision of the full armour of God, and
　　　　how you can enable them to stand in the day of evil,
　　　　　　by your power and to your glory.

(Eph. 6: 12–13)　　　　　　　　　　　　　　　　　　　*J. C.*

PENTECOST 10 (Trinity 9) The Mind of Christ

HE MADE HIMSELF NOTHING 152

We worship you, O Christ, because for our sake
  you laid aside your power and glory
  and clothed yourself in the garment of our humanity,
    to live in poverty here on earth
    and to suffer death upon the cross.
Teach us the lesson of your humility,
  and empty our lives of all pride and selfishness,
    that we may find our joy and fulfilment
in serving others in your name and for your sake.

(Phil. 2: 7, 8)   *Frank Colquhoun*

CARING FOR OTHERS' INTERESTS 153

Gracious God, as your Son our Saviour for our sake made himself nothing and became obedient to death, help us to care less for ourselves and more for the interests of others; for the sake of his name that is above every name, that holy name of 'Jesus'.

(Phil. 2: 4–10)   *J.C.*

CARRYING EACH OTHER'S BURDENS 154

Too often Lord we do not even notice the burdens that other men are carrying.
  May the Spirit give us such an awareness of them that we are ready to carry them, and so to fulfil the law of Christ.

(Gal. 6: 2)   *J.C.*

PENTECOST 11 (Trinity 10)   The Serving Community

155   INSTRUMENTS OF GOD'S PEACE

Lord, make us instruments of your peace.
    Where there is hatred, let us sow love;
    Where there is injury, pardon;
    Where there is doubt, faith;
    Where there is despair, hope;
    Where there is darkness, light;
    Where there is sadness, joy.
O Divine Master, grant that we may not so much seek
    to be consoled, as to console;
    to be understood, as to understand;
    to be loved, as to love.
For it is in giving that we receive;
    in pardoning that we are pardoned; and
    in dying that we are born to eternal life;
        through our Saviour, Jesus Christ.

After St Francis of Assisi

156   THE LOVE THAT SHOULD ABOUND

Lord, sometimes when we pray
    that our love may abound more and more
        we perhaps fail to understand what we are asking for.
We ask you then to give us that sort of love which is rooted
    in a wider knowledge and a deeper insight;
So that we may have a true discernment
    of what is best in others,
        may be pure and blameless ourselves, and
        may be filled with the fruit of that righteousness
           which comes through Jesus Christ,
        to your glory and praise.

(Phil. 1: 9–11)   *J. C.*

Thank you, O God, for the courage and faith
  of all those men and women
    who, from the time of the apostles, preached the gospel
      of the living Christ;
    those who were strong in the face of persecution;
    those who brought the good news to this land of ours;
      and
    those who have gone out to teach and to preach
      in the name of Christ their Lord.
Be with your church in every land;
    strengthen her when she is weak;
    correct her when she is in error;
    encourage her when she is failing;
    give her humility where she is proud;
  and where, day by day, she is seeking to show others
      the joy of your kingdom,
    deepen her faith in her risen Lord.
Help us each to realize that we are a part
    of your great church universal,
  and that, together with all your children,
    we can worship and adore you,
      through Jesus Christ our Lord.

Anon. (per Michael Saward)

PENTECOST 12 (Trinity 11)
The Witnessing Community

158 PURGED TO WITNESS

We are ashamed, O God, for our carelessness in worship,
  for wandering mind and thoughtless prayer.
We are ashamed that words of praise come
  so swiftly to our lips but so slowly to our hearts.
We are ashamed that we hear the name of Jesus
  but act as if he were a stranger.
Forgive us for our jealousies in the church
  and for the irritations which so easily win the day.
Forgive us for the times when we can see plainly
  what needs to be done,
  and complain that others do not do it.
Give us O Lord a vision of our church, set as it is among
  people who do not know Christ as Lord.
Give us a deepened faith,
  an understanding love,
  a ready answer,
  and an openness to the Holy Spirit.
May we so live, and so preach, that our neighbours may want
  to know the source of our joy,
  through Jesus Christ our Lord.

Anon. (per Michael Saward)

159 THE WITNESS OF THE LIVING CHURCH

Father, you give life to all, and
  eternal life to those who yield their
  allegiance to your Son:
Uphold and strengthen all who profess to serve him;
Help them to have true faith;
  to grow in it as the Holy Spirit teaches them
  through your word;
  to face the need for change in their attitudes and
  their behaviour; and
  so to radiate the light of your presence that
  individuals may be converted,
  homes transformed, and
  churches renewed.
To your glory and for Christ's sake.

Michael Saward

RENEWED TO WITNESS 160

Guide and direct, O Lord, the minds of all who work for the reshaping of our church. Restore our faith and vision. Renew our energies and love. Revive your people to new life and power. So may we live and speak for Christ before the world he came to save; for his name's sake.

Timothy Dudley-Smith

SPIRIT-FILLED TO WITNESS 161

We praise you, O God,
    because you gave the Holy Spirit to the first Christians,
        making Jesus real to them,
        teaching them the truth, and
        giving them power to witness boldly.
Fill us with the same Spirit,
    that we may know their experience and
        follow their example,
        for Jesus' sake.

Family Worship

PENTECOST 13 (Trinity 12)
The Suffering Community

'THE WAY THE MASTER WENT' 162

God our Father, whose strong Son made no answer to insult and false accusation; strengthen us to follow the pattern of his life and death, and, in the face of injustice, to trust ourselves to you, our faithful Creator and righteous Judge; for his name's sake.

(Matt. 27: 14)   *David Silk*

163   THE PRAYER OF THE JERUSALEM CHURCH

Sovereign Lord, maker of heaven, earth and sea, and of everything in them: we pray for those of your servants who are confronted by the threats of hostile men. Enable them to speak your word with great boldness; stretch out your hand to bring healing and to perform signs and wonders today, as in the early church, through the name of the same Jesus, our Lord.

(Acts 4: 24–30)   *J.C.*

164   THE PERSECUTED CHURCH

Almighty God, you have called your people to shine as lights in the world; we pray for our fellow Christians who bear their witness in difficult places, and for those who suffer persecution and imprisonment for the gospel's sake.

Uphold their faith; bless their testimony; give them freedom of spirit; and cause your Word everywhere to speed on and triumph, for the honour of our Lord and Saviour Jesus Christ.

Frank Colquhoun

165   THROUGH TROUBLES TO THE ETERNAL KINGDOM

O merciful and heavenly God, we commit to you all those who make up your church in all the world. Teach us, whom you have justified, to live by faith; bear us, by your grace, through all troubles; and bring us at last to the glory of your eternal kingdom; for the honour of our Saviour and mediator, Jesus Christ.

Anon.

PENTECOST 14 (Trinity 13)   The Family

FAMILY LOVE   **166**

We pray to you, O God,
    that those of us who are husbands or wives
      may love and serve each other;
    that those of us who are fathers or mothers
      may be fair and kind to our children;
    that those of us who are sons or daughters
      may obey and help our parents;
    that those of us who are brothers or sisters
      may share willingly and give generously; and
that all of us may grow daily more like Jesus Christ,
    who once gave himself for us,
    and is now the best friend of every family;
      for his name's sake.

(Eph. 5: 22 to 6: 4)   *C. Idle*

167
CHILDREN AS THEIR PARENTS' TRUST   **167**

Father, you have entrusted to our care
    the children of your church,
and have charged us to guide and train them
    in the way of Christ.
Help us to be faithful to our trust,
    both in our teaching and in our prayers;
    that our boys and girls may grow up
      in the knowledge of your love,
    to worship and serve you all their days
    as members of your family,
      to the honour and glory of your name.

Frank Colquhoun

168 THE HEAVENLY FATHER

We thank you, heavenly Father, for our friends and families;
May your love surround them;
May your strength protect them;
May your truth guide them;
That we may all love one another very much,
>   and love you with all our hearts and best of all;
>   for Jesus' sake.

C. Idle

169 FAMILY LIFE AND FELLOWSHIP

Father, we thank you that you have established us in families, so that we may live together, play together, work together, rejoice together, and grieve together. But above all we thank you that we are able to be members of your family the church; that through your Son Jesus Christ we are able to become your children.

We thank you that, no matter how widely spread throughout the world our Christian family may be, our hearts may be united in prayer so that we are able to share one another's burdens, rejoice in one another's blessings, and strengthen one another in the power of your Holy Spirit.

We thank you too that in your wisdom you have set aside a day when we can gather together for praise and worship and when, drawn aside from everyday living, we may be renewed together as a family by your Holy Spirit, through Jesus Christ our Lord.

Patricia Mitchell

PENTECOST 15 (Trinity 14)   Those in Authority

170 TO CAESAR AND TO GOD

Our Sovereign God, we reaffirm our commitment
>   to serve you through Jesus Christ our Redeemer,
and we thank you for every assurance you have given us
>   of your strength to keep us and
>   of your grace to guide us by the Holy Spirit.

May he give us discernment to see at all times
             where the path of duty leads us;
      for we are by your mercy
        inheritors of your heavenly kingdom, and also
        citizens of an earthly state,
             to which our Lord and Saviour has taught us
             we have a duty,
             and in which he calls us
                to live and to witness to him.
Help us then, Lord,
        to love you with all our hearts and also
        to love our neighbours as ourselves,
                    to the glory of your name.

(Matt. 22: 39)   *J. C.*

LEADERS IN SOCIETY   **171**

Lord of the universe and leader of your people,
        give wisdom to those who exercise authority among men
             or influence their opinions;
        teach them to put the good of the many
             before the advantage of the few;
        help them to love truth and
             to hate falsehood, corruption, and sinful violence;
and, above all,
        cause them to remember that he
                who would be greatest
                    must learn to be servant of all,
in the name of Jesus our Lord,
        who for our sakes made himself nothing.

(Matt. 23: 11)   *Michael Saward*

PENTECOST 16 (Trinity 15) The Neighbour

172 OUR OWN UNCONCERN FOR OTHERS

Our gracious God, we give you our thanks
    for all that you have made known to us
        from the Scriptures
    about our own need, and
    about Jesus our Saviour.
We confess our failure to be as concerned as we should
    for others who have this same need,
        but do not know him.
We ask that you will awaken each one of us
    to the responsibility we have before you
        for those who need the words of peace and love
           through Jesus Christ
        which we have a sacred duty to make known to them.
Then, Lord, give us ready hands,
           a loosened tongue, and
           an overflowing heart,
that we may faithfully serve you and our neighbour,
        to your glory.

J. C.

173 RELIEVING OTHERS' NEEDS

Almighty Father, giver of life and health, we beseech you
for the millions of people in the world who are suffering. We
acknowledge the richness of your goodness toward us, and we
pray for grace to show our thankfulness by working and giving to
relieve the needs of those who are in want. We ask it in the name
of him who is the bread of life, your Son, Jesus Christ our Lord.

Bernard Woolf

PENTECOST 17 (Trinity 16)   The Proof of Faith

AN ACT OF PENITENCE   **174**

Father, forgive the apathy and cowardice
        which hamper our witness as Christians;
    our busy occupation with lesser things
        which prevents us from seeing the great vision
            of your kingdom on earth;
    our pride and jealousy which keep us from involvement
        with others in your service;
    our many failures to mould our desires and plans into
        the shape of your loving will;
    our prejudices which hold us back from doing what you
        have called us to do in the mission of your church;
    our unreasoned fear of change and of new patterns
        of unity in ministry and worship;
    our little faith; our loss of hope; our lack of love.
Father, forgive what we have been;
        inspire what we are, and
        direct what we shall be; through Jesus Christ our
        Lord.

Alan C. Warren

THE FAITH OF THE CHURCH EXPRESSED IN ACTION   **175**

Almighty God, we pray for your blessing on all who share
    in the life and work of this church:
    in the ministry of word and sacrament,
    in teaching and pastoral care,
    in service to the diocese, the community, and
        those in need,
    in ecumenical fellowship and co-operation.
We pray for all members of the congregation,
        that in their varied callings
        they may advance your kingdom and
        bear witness to your love,
    shown in your Son Jesus Christ our Lord.

Basil Naylor

PENTECOST 18 (Trinity 17) The Offering of Life

176 THANKFUL AND MINDFUL

Lord, make us more thankful for what we have received;
  make us more content with what we have; and
  make us more mindful of other people in need.
We ask it for the sake of him who lived in poverty, our
  Saviour, Jesus Christ.

Simon H. Baynes

177 OFFERED FOR SERVICE

Heavenly Father, give to us your church here
      the word you want spoken now,
  to our community,
  to its leaders and
  to its people.
We offer ourselves to you, that, by the gift of the Holy Spirit,
      each member of your church
    may be able to live and to speak
      as an ambassador for Christ.
Make through us your appeal to men,
    that they be reconciled to you in Christ.
Use our hands for your deeds of healing and love.
Your will be done on earth, as it is in heaven—
    beginning with us,
      here in your church and in this community.
For your glory we ask it,
    in the name of Jesus Christ,
      our Saviour, and Saviour of all.

(2 Cor. 5: 20) *Jamie Wallace*

PENTECOST 19 (Trinity 18)   The Life of Faith

THE GIFT OF FAITH AT ALL TIMES   **178**

In our walk through life, bless us Lord with your gift of
    faith;
      R. For the gift of faith we ask you, Father.
Faith that you have performed wonders and miracles that
    cannot be counted;
      R. For the gift of faith we ask you, Father.
Faith that no circumstance can remove us from your
    protection;
      R. For the gift of faith we ask you, Father.
Faith that no human claim can surpass our loyalty to you;
      R. For the gift of faith we ask you, Father.
Faith that no temptation can take us beyond Christ's power
    to help us;
      R. For the gift of faith we ask you, Father.
Faith that no love can be greater than that of him who,
    while we were yet sinners, died for us;
      R. For the gift of faith we ask you, Father.
Faith to rejoice in you at all times;
      R. For the gift of faith we ask you, Father.
Lord, increase our faith, for Jesus' sake.

(Job 5: 9; Dan. 6: 10–23; Heb. 3: 18; Rom. 5: 8;
Phil. 4: 4; Matt. 7: 11; Luke 17: 5)   *J. C.*

179   PRAISE FOR THE BLESSINGS OF NEW LIFE

We worship you, we praise you, we declare our love for you,
     our God,
       because of your gift of the new life of faith.
We thank you for the new peace we have with you through
     our Lord Jesus Christ,
       who, when we were powerless, died for the ungodly.
We thank you for our new access to you
       in your majesty and holiness,
       and for the grace in which you have enabled us
       now to stand.
We thank you for our new hope of your glory,
       and for the joy it gives, even when we suffer.
We adore you for your love poured into our hearts
       by the Holy Spirit given to us, and
       for the reconciliation we have received through our
          Lord Jesus Christ,
          who died for us and is alive for evermore.

(Rom. 5: 1–11)   *J. C.*

PENTECOST 20 (Trinity 19)   **Endurance**

180   PERSEVERANCE

Teach us, good Lord, to serve you as you deserve;
       to give, and not to count the cost;
       to fight, and not to heed the wounds;
       to toil, and not to seek for rest;
       to labour, and not to ask for any reward
          but that of knowing that we do your will;
          through Jesus Christ our Lord.

St Ignatius Loyola

FOR THE HOUR OF SUFFERING 181

There are times, O God, when the burdens and sufferings of the hour seem to us more solid and real than the words of your promises.

Give us and all your people at these times your peace, which transcends all understanding and will guard our hearts and minds in Christ Jesus.

Assure us and all your people that the hope stored up for us in heaven is that which is real and enduring.

Convince us and all your people that present sufferings are not worth comparing with the glory that is to be revealed in us, who know that in all things God works for the good of those who love him.

(Rom. 8: 18, 28; Phil. 4: 7; Col. 1: 5)   J.C.

FIT FOR SERVICE IN THE KINGDOM 182

We thank you, Lord God, for all who declare their readiness to follow Jesus wherever he leads.

Give strength and faith in the hour of testing that they and we may not look back, and may be truly fit for service in your kingdom;
              through Jesus Christ our Lord.

(Luke 9: 57–62)   J.C.

PENTECOST 21 (Trinity 20) The Christian Hope

183 THE HOPE WE SHARE

We praise you, O God our Father,
    for the hope of our calling:
    for the victory of our Lord Jesus Christ,
      who has broken the power of death and
      brought life and immortality to light through the gospel;
    for the eternal home which he has gone to prepare for
      us, and
    for his promise to come again and receive us to himself;
    for the great multitude which no man can number,
      out of every nation,
    who stand before his throne and
    with whom in our Lord we for evermore are one.

(2 Tim. 1: 10; John 14: 2–3; Rev. 7: 9) *Frank Colquhoun*

184 THE HOPE FROM WHICH FAITH AND LOVE SPRING

We praise you, our God, for the word of truth
    which you have made known to us
    and in which we have heard of the hope
      stored up for us in heaven.
Give us such assurance of this hope
    that our love may be deepened for all your people
    and our faith strengthened in Christ Jesus, our Lord.

(Col. 1: 4–5) *J. C.*

PENTECOST 22 (Trinity 21)   The Two Ways

THE UNSTABLE   185

Have mercy, O Lord,
    on all those whose judgment of truth is rooted
        in the opinions of others;
    on all who are swayed by pressure groups to do things
        which they themselves would never think of doing;
    on all whose lack of purpose,
        lack of conviction,
        lack of stability or
        lack of employment
    makes them available to the purposes of others
    and delivers them as a weapon
        into the hands of evil men.
Give to all people everywhere, O Lord, a spirit of
    responsibility and discernment,
    and make them more ready to seek for the truth and less
    ready to believe a lie;
        through Jesus Christ our Lord.

Dick Williams

FOLLOWING THE LORD'S WAY   186

Plant in us, Lord, the desire always to follow your way.
Help us to hear and obey the Spirit's voice
    when we are about to turn aside from it,
        through careless lack of prayer
        or through wilful disobedience.
Restrain us when we want to rush ahead
    without waiting for your guidance.
And give us such an understanding of how large
    are the blessings you intend for us
    that we do not settle back into a state
        of lazy contentment
    with what is short of your loving purpose,
        for Christ's sake.

J. C.

LAST SUNDAY AFTER PENTECOST
Citizens of Heaven

187   THE PROMISE OF HIS COMING

Deliver us, Lord Jesus, from being so taken up with the worries and tasks of daily life, and also with its riches and pleasures, that we overlook the promise of your coming and forget that our citizenship is in heaven.

Fill us with eager expectation of your return; help us to press on daily to take hold of that for which you have taken hold of us.

To the eternal glory of your name.

(Phil. 3: 7–21; Luke 8: 14; 2 Pet. 3: 4)   *J.C.*

188   CHARACTERISTICS OF CITIZENSHIP

Father, in whose name we are joined in common,
    here and throughout the world:
  we pray that we and all your family
    may from your glorious riches
    and through the Spirit
  be so strengthened in our inner being
    that Christ may dwell in our hearts by faith.
May we all be so rooted and established in love
  that we are enabled to grasp
    how immense is the love of Christ
    and even to know this love
    that surpasses knowledge,
  so that it is with your fullness
    that we are daily being filled,
      even to the measure of the fullness of God,
to whom be glory in the church and in Christ Jesus,
      for ever and ever!

(Eph. 3: 15–21)   *J.C.*

OTHER OCCASIONS

BAPTISM

THOSE ABOUT TO BRING CHILDREN TO BAPTISM   189

God our Father,
    from whom every family in heaven and on earth
      takes its name:
Be present to bless the families of the children
    who are soon to be baptized
    as members of your church.
Help parents and godparents
    to see the meaning of your saving gospel;
    to make their promises sincerely and without reserve;
    to enter into commitment to pray for these children; and
    to teach them about you.
So may they and the children together share
    in your gift of eternal life,
      through Jesus Christ our Lord.

C. Idle

A PRAYER FOR THE WHOLE CONGREGATION   190

Sovereign Lord, help us
    and all who are baptized into Christ's death
    to consider ourselves dead to sin;
    to walk in newness of life; and
    to be united in resurrection with him,
      our Lord and Saviour Jesus Christ.

(Rom. 6: 3–11)   *J. C.*

191 THE UPBRINGING OF CHILDREN

Heavenly Father, we pray for children who in baptism
                have entered upon the Christian life
        and for all who will share in their upbringing.
Give your blessing now and in the times ahead
                to parents and godparents,
                to brothers and sisters,
                to teachers and school-friends, and
                to all of us who have welcomed these children
                        into the household of faith.
May they grow in body,
                in mind and
                in love for you;
May each fulfil your loving purpose in life;
In the name of the friend of children,
        our Saviour Jesus Christ.

J. C.

192 FOR GODPARENTS (AFTER THE BAPTISM)

God and Father of us all:
        we pray for those who
        in the presence of this congregation
        have undertaken the responsibility
        of serving as godparents.
Help them by your grace to fulfil their duties,
        and keep them faithful in prayer,
                that their godchildren may grow up
                in the knowledge of your love and
                in the faith of our Lord Jesus Christ,
                and may serve and worship you all their days
                in the fellowship of the church,
                        to the glory of your name.

Frank Colquhoun

193 THANKSGIVING

Heavenly Father, we thank you that in uniting us with
Christ in our baptism you have made us one with all members of
your worldwide church.

Accept our praise that you have made us new creatures; that the old life is over, and the new life has begun.

Help us to glorify you by daily dying to sin and rising to righteousness, in fellowship with all Christ's people everywhere and by the constant empowering of your Holy Spirit.

(2 Cor. 5: 17, I Pet. 2: 24)   *Frank Colquhoun*

CONFIRMATION

THOSE PREPARING FOR CONFIRMATION   194

Heavenly Father, Lord of the church:
    we join in our prayer to you
        for all those now preparing for confirmation.
By your Holy Spirit may they have
    a growing understanding of your word,
    a growing commitment to their Saviour,
    a growing experience of you, and
    a growing awareness of the fellowship of your church.
May they then be resolved to confess Christ crucified, and
        strengthened to serve him until their lives' end,
            to the glory of your name.

J. C.

THE NEWLY CONFIRMED   195

Heavenly Father, you have given your servants grace
    boldly to confess their faith and
    to dedicate themselves to your service.
Help them to put Christ first in every part of their lives,
        to meet him regularly at his table and in your word,
        and to grow in the knowledge of his love.
Strengthen them daily by your Holy Spirit.
Keep them as faithful members of your church
    all the days of their lives,
        always giving thanks to you
            for victory through our Lord Jesus Christ.

(I Cor. 15: 57)   *Martin Parsons*

196   RESPONSIBILITY OF THE WHOLE CHURCH

We thank you, our God and Father, for those who in confirmation have made confession of their faith and have been welcomed into the communicant life of the Christian family in this place.

Help us each one, by our prayers, our friendship and our example, to encourage them in the way of Christ, that they may fully grow up into him and continue steadfastly in the worship and fellowship of the Church, to the glory of your name; through Jesus Christ our Lord.

Frank Colquhoun

197   CONFIRMATION CLASSES

We commit to you, heavenly Father,
    the confirmation classes in our parish.
May those who instruct and those who learn be enabled
        to have an understanding of each other, and
        to be together led and taught by your Holy Spirit.
So may all be strengthened
    as members of the one body of Christ,
    in whose name we pray.

J. C.

MORNING

198   DAILY STRENGTHENING BY THE HOLY SPIRIT

Into your hands, O Lord, we commend ourselves and all who are dear to us this day.

Be with us as we go out and as we come in; strengthen us for the work you have prepared for us to do.

Grant that we may be filled with your Holy Spirit, and so may walk worthy of our high calling and joyfully achieve all you want us to do; through Jesus Christ our Lord.

Bishop Theodore Woods

Go with us, O Lord, into this unknown day, and help us in all the duties and pleasures which lie ahead.

Make us prepared for the unexpected things as well as for those which we know will take place; keep us watchful against the sudden attack of temptation, that it may not take us unawares.

Make us quick to seize every opportunity of helping someone who is in need. Keep us ready for the request we could not foresee, and the problem we did not anticipate.

So grant, O Lord, that this day may be one in which we prove your help in our lives, and find true happiness in our hearts, through Jesus Christ our Lord.

John Eddison

EVENING

ENCOUNTER WITH THE LORD   200

Creator God and gracious Lord:
  It was in the cool of the day that you came to Adam and Eve,
    and in the evening that they confessed their sin;
  It was at evening that the dove returned to Noah
    with the olive-leaf that was your sign
      of new hope and a fresh beginning;
  It was toward evening that Jesus completed his suffering
    for our redemption,
    and as darkness came that his risen presence
    and his peace dispelled his disciples' fear.
Loving Saviour:
  At the end of the day may we
    be overjoyed that you are among us, and
    be strengthened now by your Holy Spirit to serve you
      as you will send us in your name.

Adapted by J. C. from 'Am Abend, da es kühle war'
in J. S. Bach's 'St Matthew Passion'
(Gen. 3: 8–13 & 8: 10–11; Luke 23: 44; John 19: 30 & 20: 19–22)

201 CONFESSION

Forgive us, O heavenly Father,
 for all that has made this day less enjoyable than it should
  have been—for ourselves and for others—
 for times when we have been proud, selfish, or lazy;
  when we have forsaken duty for pleasure;
  when we have not loved you as we ought.
We ask
 that we may learn by our failures, and
 that what have been stumbling-blocks today
   may tomorrow be stepping-stones along our way.
Bless us all tonight;
Grant us refreshing sleep;
May we rise tomorrow ready
 to follow you more closely, and
 to serve you better;
   through Jesus Christ our Lord.

John Eddison

202 THOSE WHO ARE AWAKE WHILE WE SLEEP

We thank you, O Lord,
 for bringing us safely to the end of another day;
 for protecting us from accident and illness; and
 for providing us with all our daily needs.
We thank you for the gift of sleep,
 and we ask that you will use it tonight
 to refresh us in mind and body, and
 to prepare us for all that tomorrow holds in store.
Finally, we commend to you all those who this night
  will enjoy little or no sleep—
 those who work while we rest;
 those responsible for our security; and
 those who are kept awake
  through the long hours of darkness
   by pain, anxiety, or sorrow.
O Lord, in blessing us, bless them also,
 and may your peace guard their hearts and minds,
  through Jesus Christ our Lord.

John Eddison

SEASONS OF THE YEAR

SPRING 203

We see around us O Lord the dawn of nature—buds beginning to break and birds to nest. We thank you for the beauty of these things, and that once again nature is awaking from the long, cold months of sleep.

May we too, O Lord, awake to righteousness and bestir ourselves to do your will. Fill us with new energy and new enthusiasm, that we may approach all we have to do in a fresh and lively spirit, through Jesus Christ our Lord.

John Eddison

SUMMER 204

We thank you dear Lord for the warmth and sunshine of long summer days, for the beauty of the countryside, and for all the sights and sounds of nature.

Help us to benefit from these days. May they speak to us of the warmth of your love.

Bless those who use them for holidays, for rest and recreation. Bless particularly those who cannot use them in this way; those whose work binds them to city or factory; those who labour at night; those who are handicapped by poverty or sickness.

So grant that in our own happiness we may ever be mindful of the needs of others, through Jesus Christ our Lord.

John Eddison

AUTUMN 205

O Lord, the fading flowers and falling leaves remind us that once more summer is past and over; and though we watch its departure with regret, yet we rejoice in the beauty of autumn.

Help us to trace your loving kindness to us not only in the sunshine, but also in the shadows, and to remember that sometimes disappointment, trouble, and sorrow are in truth thin disguises of your love, and ways by which you would bind us more closely to yourself, through Jesus Christ our Lord.

John Eddison

206   WINTER

We thank you, O Lord, for the seasons of the year, and especially today for the changing moods of winter—for storm and sunshine, wind and rain, frost and ice and snow, for brown fields and bare trees. We thank you too for the comfort and warmth of bed, for food, clothing, companionship, and exercise.

But we pray for all those who must face the winter months without the benefit of these things: for the disabled and sick, for the very old and the poor, for the lonely and the unloved. Grant them your help, O Lord, and may we, so far as we are able, try to relieve them in their need, through Jesus Christ our Lord.

John Eddison

SEED-TIME (Rogation)

207   OUR DEPENDENCE ON GOD'S GIVING

Lord God, as we sow seed, or plant,
          hoping for a rich harvest,
     we pray that we may be delivered
          from thinking that this comes
               wholly of its own accord, or
               simply due to our efforts.
Teach us again
          that sun and rain are your gifts,
          that by ourselves we can do nothing and
          that we are stewards of your creation.
In your mercy, grant us
          favourable crops,
          trusting and thankful hearts, and
          wise and fair use of your gifts,
                         for Jesus' sake.

J. C.

HARVEST

OUR RESPONSE TO GOD'S PROVISION 208

Almighty and everlasting God, who has given us the fruits of the earth in their seasons and has crowned the year with your goodness:

Give us grateful hearts that we may in truth thank you for all your love and mercy, and may bring glory to your name in our lives; through Jesus Christ our Lord.

Bishop John Dowden

THE RIGHT USE OF GOD'S GIFTS 209

We thank you, God, for the harvest of all good things;
for making plants to grow in the earth;
for giving us the strength to work;
for supplying the food we have each day.
Teach us to use your gifts fairly and generously,
and to remember that you gave them to us:
in the name of Jesus Christ.

C. Idle

MOTHERING SUNDAY

210 THANKSGIVINGS AND INTERCESSIONS

Loving God, we thank you that Jesus enjoyed a mother's love and grew up within a family.

We thank you for the homes where we were born, and for the care and affection of our mothers.

We pray for all mothers today:

> for expectant mothers, especially those awaiting the birth of their first child;
>
> for those who have young or ~~handicapped~~ *disabled* children, and who get tired and harassed with so much to do;
>
> for those who are anxious because their children are growing up and seem to be growing away from them;
>
> for those who feel a sense of emptiness as their children marry and leave home;
>
> for those who are elderly and may feel unwanted;
>
> for those who have no husband to share their responsibilities—the widowed, the divorced, and the unmarried mothers.

All women called to nurture

We pray also for those who have been denied the privilege of motherhood—those who cannot have children of their own, and those who have never had the opportunity to marry.

Finally we pray for those who are closest to us:

> may we love and care for them
> as we ourselves have been loved and helped.

We ask it for your love's sake.

John Searle

FATHER'S DAY

211 HUMAN FATHERS AND THE HEAVENLY FATHER

Loving God, we thank you especially today
> for our fathers,
> for their love, care and protection,
> for all they do that we may have
> > food, clothes, and homes,
> for play-times and holiday-times with them.

We remember the boys and girls who have no father,
and ask that someone will look after them
and make them happy.
We thank you that you gave your Son Jesus for us,
and we ask that we may be helped
lovingly to trust him as our Saviour,
joyfully to know you as our heavenly Father, and
gladly to live lives that please you,
by the help of your Holy Spirit.

Adapted from John D. Searle

REMEMBRANCE SUNDAY

YESTERDAY'S WARS AND TODAY'S NEEDS 212

O heavenly Lord, in whose hands are the nations and peoples
of the earth:
We thank you for the deliverance from evil which you gave
through those who fought, suffered, endured and died in
two world wars;
We thank you too for all the evidences of your gracious hand
upon our nation.
We pray for those who still bear the scars of war,
in body or mind;
Help us to show the love of Christ
in our attitudes towards them;
We pray for all peoples who are now at variance with one
another, asking that they may be ready
to admit what is sinful on their own part, and
to forgive what they think to be sinful in others;
We pray too that they and all men may,
by the working of the Holy Spirit,
be brought to know for themselves
the whole gospel of Jesus Christ,
who, by dying for our sins,
showed that no man can have greater love
than that of laying down his life for others.
All this we ask in the name of him who is
the Prince of Peace.

(John 15: 13)

J. C.

213   FOR USE IN NORTHERN IRELAND

Lord of the nations, we remember before you today
  those who have given their lives in defence of
    their homeland, and
    their people,
  whether in two world wars, or at the hands of terrorists.
Our hearts are sad as we remember
  their suffering,
  their families' grief, and
  our own readiness to look only to our own interests
    and not also to the interests of others.
Move us Lord to express the reality behind our words
  by our loving care for those who have survived them but
    who carry the continuing burden of bereavement,
and also
  by both resolving and acting
    to make this land a place marked by
      justice,
      mutual respect, and
      compassion
    among all its people.
So may Christ be glorified in all who profess his name.

(Phil. 2: 4)   *J. C.*

CHURCH ANNIVERSARY OR FESTIVAL

---

214   AN ANNIVERSARY

Great is your faithfulness, O God our Father,
  and great is our joy at this time
    as we celebrate this anniversary.
We thank you for the witness this church has maintained
  down the years,
    as a centre of Christian worship and witness,
                      teaching and service.
We thank you for all who have loyally served it
      as clergy and laity,
    for all who have gone out from it
      in obedience to your call, and
    for the continuance of its life and work today.

Accept our thanksgiving, O God;
    multiply your blessings upon us today;
    and lead us forward in the power of your Spirit
        to fresh ventures of faith in the days to come;
            through Jesus Christ our Lord.

Frank Colquhoun

PATRONAL FESTIVAL 215

Almighty God, to whose glory we celebrate the dedication of this house of prayer: we give you thanks for the fellowship of those who have worshipped in this place; and we pray that all who seek you here may find you, and be filled with your joy and peace; through Jesus Christ our Lord.

Episcopal Church, USA

A FLOWER FESTIVAL 216

We thank you, dear Lord, for the beauty of flowers
    and the pleasure they give to us.
Thank you for the gift of a child's posy,
    gathered from the hedgerows or the garden.
Thank you for flowers given as a love-token.
Thank you for the bowls and vases of flowers
    that make our homes bright.
Thank you for the flowers that beautify our church,
    and for the hands that arranged them;
        in Jesus' name.

Beryl Bye

217   FLOWERS IN CHURCH

Lord Jesus, we remember that you have told us to consider
  how the lilies of the field grow.
We thank you for the glory of their Creator, and
                    for our delight in his creation.
You have taught us
      how wonderful is the Father's care
          for these passing beauties of nature,
      but also how infinitely greater
          is his loving care for us.
Help us, then, to learn from the flowers
    that we see around us today,
          seeking first God's kingdom and his righteousness.
Help us not to worry about tomorrow,
          but instead to rest in his promise and his power,
          and so to glorify him in our lives.

(Matt. 6: 28–34)   *J. C.*

HOME MISSION

218   BEFORE A PARISH MISSION

O God, we thank you for your word of hope:
      that coins and sheep are found as well as lost,
      that prodigals return to a welcome,
      that there is joy in heaven over one sinner who repents,
          and that years which the locust has eaten can be restored.
We thank you for the word of hope
      made actual and accessible to us
          in Jesus Christ your Son.
Give grace that we may lay hold of the Good News
      and be found in him.

(Luke 15: 4–24; Joel 2: 25)   *Jamie Wallace*

Lord Jesus, Lord of the church,
    as you have led us to undertake mission in our parish,
    so we ask you to help us to continue
        to look for your leading and
        to depend on your power.
We need, and pray for, your blessing on all who work here
    in your name:
        on those who lead us in prayer groups;
        on those responsible for publicity;
        on those who serve as organizers and stewards;
        on those who teach and learn how to give counsel;
        on those who go to schools and factories;
        on those who visit in the homes of the parish;
        on those who try to bring friends and neighbours
            to the church;
        on those who sing in choirs or as soloists;
        on those who speak or preach;
        on those who help enquirers.
Our Saviour and Lord, grant
    that those of us who have grown cold
        may find faith and love re-kindled;
    that those who have burdens may find them lifted;
    that those who are bound by sin
        may repent and find new life;
    that in the days and in the years ahead your church here
        may be marked by
            greater desire to study and to heed your word;
            greater love for you in joining at your table and
            greater joy in serving you, to your glory.

                                                    J. C.

(The itemized petitions in the second clause
may be omitted or shortened as appropriate)

MISSIONERS

We praise you, gracious Lord, for the message of your love
    for sinful men,
        as it has been given to us in the scriptures.
We thank you for the Holy Spirit,
        who has spoken through them to men in every age.
We ask that he may speak now
        to those entrusted with making this message known, and
        to those who hear it proclaimed;
    that many may be brought to rejoice in new life,
        by faith in the only Lord and Saviour, Jesus Christ.

J. C.

THE CHURCH AT WORSHIP

THE APPROACH TO WORSHIP

PREPARATION FOR WORSHIP 221

Forgive us, O Lord, we beseech you,
  for all our past sins and failures,
and help us now to worship you
  in spirit and in truth.
Take from us all wandering thoughts;
incline our hearts and minds to do your will;
help us to sing your praise with all our hearts,
and to listen to your word with open ears.
May we then go forth from here as those
  who 'have been with Jesus',
    in whose name we pray.

(Acts 4: 13)   *John Eddison*

THE PARISH CHURCH 222

God our Father, we thank you for this house of prayer
        in which you bless your family on its pilgrimage.
So quicken our consciences by your holiness,
      nourish our minds by your truth,
      purify our imaginations by your beauty, and
      open our hearts to your love
          that, in the surrender of our wills to your purpose,
              the world may be renewed in Christ Jesus our
              Lord.

After William Temple

AN OPENING EXHORTATION

223   GOD'S WORD AND OUR RESPONSE

Brothers and sisters in Christ, the Bible urges us repeatedly to admit and confess our many sins and evil ways. We must not try to hide them from Almighty God, our heavenly Father. We must confess them with a humble, lowly, penitent, and obedient heart, so that we may find forgiveness through God's limitless goodness and mercy.

We ought always humbly to admit our sins before God, but specially when we come together—

> to worship;
> to give thanks for the great benefits which we have received from him;
> to offer him the praise which is his due;
> to hear his most holy word; and
> to ask him to supply continually the needs of our bodies and our souls.

I urge you therefore, all who are gathered here, to accompany me with a pure heart and humble voice, as we draw near to God's throne of grace together.

From a modern form of the Prayer Book Exhortation,
prepared for the Diocese of Central Tanganyika

CONFESSION AND PARDON

224   RELEASE FROM THE BONDAGE OF SIN

O God, whose nature and character it is
    ever to be merciful and forgiving:
Hear us as we pray to you;
Though we find ourselves tied and bound
    by our own sinfulness,
Set us free from this bondage,
    by your great mercy and
    by Jesus Christ, our Mediator and Advocate.

Adapted from Book of Common Prayer

225   DEEPER UNDERSTANDING

Heavenly Father, we thank you
    for sending your Son to die on the cross
    that we might be forgiven.
Help us to understand both
    the extent of our sin and
    the greatness of his love,
        so that we may
            trust him as our Saviour and
            serve him as our Lord.

M. H. Botting's collection

226   HALF-HEARTED DISCIPLESHIP

Heavenly Father, we confess
    how often we disobey what we know to be your will;
    how often we forget you and leave you out of our lives;
    how often we are too blind to know our sins,
            too proud to admit them,
            too indifferent to make amends.
We confess how half-hearted and unworthy we are
    as members of your church and
    as your witnesses before men.
In your mercy, O Lord,
    forgive us our sins, and
    give us honest, humble, and penitent hearts;
        for the sake of our Saviour Jesus Christ.

After William Temple

INTERCESSION

227   A PRAYER FOR ALL WHO ARE IN NEED

Eternal God, to whom all may come through your Son:
    lay your healing hand upon those who are sick;
    make your loving presence known
        to those who are lonely;
    give your strengthening power to those who are fearful;
    may those who lack be filled;
        those who mourn be comforted;
        those who worry be calmed; and
        those who seek forgiveness find it in Jesus Christ;
Through whom we pray.

Michael Saward

228   A PRAYER OF THE EASTERN CHURCH

Be mindful, O Lord,
    of us your people who are present
        together here in this place, and
    of those who are absent
        through age, frailty or sickness.
We commend the children to your care,
        the young to your guidance,
        the married to your enriching,
        the aged to your support,
        the faint-hearted to your strengthening power,
        the scattered to your shepherd's love, and
        the wandering to your call to repent and be
            forgiven.
Journey with all travellers;
    help the bereaved;
    release the addicted;
    heal the sick.
Bring assurance to all who are passing through
        trouble,
        need, or
        anxiety.

Remember for good
    all those who love us,
    those who care nothing for us, and
    those who have asked us (unworthy as we are)
        to pray for them.
There are surely some whom we have forgotten,
    but you, Lord, will surely remember them;
For you are
    the helper of the helpless,
    the saviour of the lost,
    the refuge for the wanderer, and
    the healer of the sick.
Since you know each one's need,
        and hear every prayer,
    we commend each one to
        your merciful grace and
        your everlasting love.
Grant to us that together
    we may praise your great name,
        now and for ever.

Based by J. C. on the Anaphora of St Basil the Great

Almighty and everliving God:
    you have taught us to pray,
        interceding and giving thanks for all men.
We humbly ask that in your mercy you will
    [accept our offerings and]*
    receive our prayers to your divine majesty.
We pray for the worldwide church,
        that it may always be inspired with the spirit
            of truth, unity and concord.
    May all who profess your holy name
        agree in the truth of your holy word, and
        live in unity, godliness and love.
We pray that you will protect and guide all Christian rulers
    [and especially Elizabeth our Queen]†
    that they may be enabled
        to administer justice faithfully and impartially,
        to take their stand against evil,
        to declare their true faith, and
        to uphold the right.
Give your grace to all bishops and ministers
    that by their lives and teaching they may
            make known your true and living word,
    and that they may rightly administer your sacraments.
Give your grace also to all your people,
        especially to us in this congregation,
    so that we may
        hear your holy word with reverence,
        receive its teaching with humility, and
        serve you all our days in holiness.
We commend to your goodness, Lord,
        all who are in trouble, sorrow, need, sickness,
        or any other burden of this fleeting life,
    and we ask you to strengthen and help them.
As we thank you for all your servants
        who have passed from this life
            trusting and serving you,
    we ask that you will give us such grace
        to follow their good examples
    that we may share with them
        in your heavenly kingdom.

* This phrase should be omitted when there are no alms.
† This phrase is for use only in Northern Ireland.

Grant all this, our Father,
    for the sake of Jesus Christ, who alone
        is our Mediator,
        intercedes for us, and
        is our Lord and Saviour.

Adapted by J. C. from the 'Prayer for the Church Militant'
in the Book of Common Prayer

HUMAN NEED AND HUMAN LOVE   230

Hear our prayer, O God,
    for all who are ill, and all whose vocation is healing;
    for those in trouble,
        and those whose business is helping.
Raise us all up to the high calling of being good neighbours,
    in the name and the Spirit of Jesus Christ your Son.

Jamie Wallace

A PRAYER TO SUM UP OUR REQUESTS   231

Heavenly Father, we remember thankfully
    that Jesus spoke to his disciples,
    promising them that whatever they would ask
        in his name they would receive, and
    assuring them that their joy would be complete:
We therefore now bring together before you in his name
        all our intercessions and requests;
We pray that what we have asked in faith and according to
    your will may indeed be granted
        in whatever way your love and wisdom see
            best meets our needs, and
            most sets forth your glory.

(John 16: 24)   *Adapted from Book of Common Prayer*

BEFORE THE SERMON

232   HE WHO SPEAKS AND THOSE WHO HEAR

May the words of my mouth,
  and the meditations of all our hearts,
be now and always pleasing in your sight,
  O Lord, our strength, and our Redeemer.

(Ps. 19: 14)

233   THE WORD

Grant, O Lord, that
    in the written word,
    and through the spoken word,
    we may each one behold the living Word,
        our Saviour Jesus Christ.

Simon H. Baynes

HOLY COMMUNION

234   PREPARATION OF HEART

Lord Jesus, help us to draw near to your table
    with obedient hearts,
        in response to your own invitation;
    with penitent hearts,
        acknowledging our need of forgiveness;
    with expectant hearts,
        knowing that you are present to meet with us;
    with grateful hearts,
        as those for whom your body was broken,
                your blood shed.
Make us ready
    to receive all that you have for us, and
    to give all of ourselves to you;
            for your great love's sake.

Frank Colquhoun

THE LIVING BREAD   235

Lord God of our fathers, you feed your children with the true manna, the living Bread from heaven; let this holy food support us through our earthly pilgrimage until we come to the place where there is neither hunger nor thirst; through Christ our Lord.

David Silk

HE WHO CALLS US   236

Lord, the feast is yours,
    not ours.
It is your table to which we come,
    to be your guests.
It is your presence we seek,
    your body and blood of which we partake.
Help us to draw near with expectant hearts
                and a living faith,
    to receive as from your hands
                the bread of life,
                the cup of salvation, and so
to find refreshment, strength and peace;
    for your love's sake.

Frank Colquhoun

THE FAMILY   237

God our Father, whose Son at table offered himself as the innocent Lamb, and gave us this memorial of his passion until the end of time: feed your people, and strengthen them in holiness, that the family of mankind may live in the light of one faith in one communion of love, through the same Christ our Lord.

David Silk

238   COMMUNION WITH ONE ANOTHER IN CHRIST

O God, in this eucharist you have united us in the bond of peace; deepen our communion one with another in Christ, and grant that, through the work of your Spirit within us, we may daily increase in the knowledge of your love, and learn to love our brothers with the love you have shown in Jesus Christ our Lord.

Adapted by David Silk

239   THANKS FOR ALL THAT IS SIGNIFIED

Lord Jesus Christ, we thank you for giving us
   the sacrament of Holy Communion, to be to us and
    your whole church
       a memorial of your passion,
       a pledge of your redeeming love,
       a means of spiritual grace, and
       a foretaste of the heavenly banquet.
Make these things real to us, O Christ,
   when we partake of the sacrament.
Above all, make yourself real to us,
      as our living Saviour and Lord,
      ever to be honoured, worshipped and adored.

Frank Colquhoun

240   AFTER THE COMMUNION

Thank you, Father, for all the words
    which we have said and sung and heard:
   the story and celebration of your power,
   the faith of the psalmists,
   the hope of the prophets,
   the joy of the first Christians,
     witnesses of Christ's resurrection
      to whom he was made known, risen and alive,
       in the breaking of bread.

Once we are out of church again, help us
    to know your power,
        your victory and
        your presence with us,
    to bear Christ's cross and share Christ's victory
        every day of the week,
    to be involved with you
        in the redemption of the world.
Almighty Father, show us how,
        and make it happen,
        through Christ's grace,
           for we ask it in his name.

Jamie Wallace

MUSIC AND SINGING

BEFORE HYMN-SINGING   241

Lord of all joy, fill us now with your Spirit;
    grant that in singing your praise
        we may strengthen one another,
        and that our music may be made in our hearts,
    as we give thanks to you for everything
        in the name of our Lord Jesus Christ.

(Eph. 5: 18–20)   *J. C.*

THANKSGIVING FOR MUSIC   242

Father, we thank you
    for the many ways we can express ourselves,
        and especially for the gift of music.
We thank you for the way it can describe every emotion—
        joy and delight,
        melancholy and sadness,
        wonder and worship,
        love and devotion.
We thank you that music can soothe the soul
    and bring solace to those who mourn.
We praise you that we can give thanks to you for everything,
    singing and making melody in our heart,
        in the name of Jesus Christ our Lord.

(Eph. 5: 19–20)   *Patricia Mitchell*

243   CHOIR MEMBERS

Lord God Almighty,
  all heaven proclaims your glory with ceaseless voice.
We pray that you will now accept
  the praises of your church here.
Pour upon those who lead our worship
  such a spirit of faith, reverence and joy
    as shall lift to you both their song and our lives
      through Jesus Christ our Lord.

(Rev. 4: 8–11)   *Eric Milner-White*

VALEDICTIONS

244   THE ENCOURAGEMENT OF CHRIST'S COMING

The Lord himself will come down from heaven,
  with a loud command,
    with the voice of the archangel, and
    with the trumpet call of God,
  and the dead in Christ will rise first.
After that, we who are still alive and are left
  will be caught up with them . . .
    to meet the Lord. . . .
  And so we will be with the Lord for ever.
Therefore encourage each other with these words.

(1 Thess. 4: 16–18)   (*NIV*)

245   GREAT JOY IN THE LAST DAY

To him who is able
  to keep you from falling and
  to present you before his glorious presence
    without fault
    and with great joy—

to the only God our Saviour
be glory, majesty, power and authority,
    through Jesus Christ our Lord,
before all ages,
now and
for evermore! Amen.

(Jude 24–5)   (*NIV*)

ETERNAL GLORY TRANSCENDS THE 'LITTLE WHILE'   **246**

The God of all grace,
        who called you to his eternal glory in Christ,
after you have suffered a little while,
        will himself restore you
            and make you strong, firm and steadfast.
To him be the power for ever and ever. Amen.

(1 Pet. 5: 10, 11)   (*NIV*)

ENCOURAGEMENT AND STRENGTH   **247**

May our Lord Jesus Christ himself
    and God our Father,
        who loved us and by his grace gave us
            eternal encouragement and good hope,
        encourage and strengthen you
            in every good deed and word.

(2 Thess. 2: 16–17)   (*NIV*)

THE POWER AND THE GLORY AMONG MEN   **248**

Now to him who is able to do
        immeasurably more than all we ask or imagine,
    according to his power that is at work within us,
    to him be glory
        in the church and
        in Christ Jesus
throughout all generations, for ever and ever! Amen.

(Eph. 3: 20–1)   (*NIV*)

249   GOD, THE LORD OF ALL

O the depth of the riches,
                the wisdom and
                the knowledge of God!
How unsearchable his judgments,
                and his paths beyond tracing out! . . .
From him and through him and to him
                are all things.
To him be the glory for ever! Amen.

(Rom. 11: 33, 36)   (*NIV*)

250   A TRINITARIAN CHARGE

Be very careful how you live . . .,
                making the most of every opportunity.
Be filled with the Spirit . . .,
                always giving thanks to God the Father for everything,
                in the name of our Lord Jesus Christ.

(Eph. 5: 15–20)   (*NIV*)

251   ON SERVICE FOR CHRIST

Be on your guard;
                stand firm in the faith;
                be men of courage;
                be strong.
Do everything in love.
The grace of the Lord Jesus be with you.

(1 Cor. 16: 13, 14, 23)   (*NIV*)

252   THE HOPE THAT OVERFLOWS

May the God of hope fill you with great joy and peace
                as you trust in him,
                so that you may overflow with hope
                by the power of the Holy Spirit.

(Rom. 15: 13)   (*NIV*)

THE LOVE THAT OVERFLOWS 253

May the Lord make your love increase and overflow
    for each other
    and for everyone else. . . .
May he give you inner strength
    that you may be blameless and holy . . .
    when our Lord Jesus comes.

(1 Thess. 3: 12, 13)   *(NIV)*

DISCERNMENT AND BLAMELESSNESS 254

[May] your love . . . abound more and more
    in knowledge and depth of insight,
so that you may be able to discern what is best
and may be pure and blameless
    until the day of Christ,
filled with the fruit of righteousness
    that comes through Christ—
        to the glory and praise of God.

(Phil. 1: 9–11)   *(NIV)*

HOLINESS 255

Prepare your minds for action;
    be self-controlled;
    set your hope fully on the grace to be given you
        when Jesus Christ is revealed. . . .
Just as he who called you is holy,
    so be holy in all you do.

(1 Pet. 1: 13, 15)   *(NIV)*

A NEW CREATION 256

What counts is a new creation.
Peace and mercy to all who follow this rule,
    even to the Israel of God. . . .
The grace of our Lord Jesus Christ
    be with your spirit, brothers. Amen.

(Gal. 6: 15, 16, 18)   *(NIV)*

257   COMMISSIONED BY CHRIST

    Jesus said, 'Peace be with you! As the Father has sent me, I
am sending you. . . . Receive the Holy Spirit.'

(John 20: 21, 22)   (*NIV*)

258   THE INDWELLING CHRIST

Let the peace of Christ rule in your hearts,
    since, as members of one body,
        you were called to peace.
  And be thankful.
Let the word of Christ dwell in you richly. . . .
And whatever you do, . . .
    do it all in the name of the Lord Jesus,
      giving thanks to God the Father through him.

(Col. 3: 15–17)   (*NIV*)

259   THE WILL OF GOD AT WORK

May the God of peace,
    who through the blood of the eternal covenant
        brought back from the dead our Lord Jesus,
            that great Shepherd of the sheep,
    equip you with everything good
      for doing his will,
    and may he work in us
      what is pleasing to him,
        through Jesus Christ,
            to whom be glory for ever and ever. Amen.

(Heb. 13: 20–1)   (*NIV*)

260   HUMBLE AND TRUSTING

Humble yourselves . . . under God's mighty hand,
    that he may lift you up in due time.
Cast all your anxiety on him
    because he cares for you. . . .
Peace to all of you who are in Christ.

(1 Pet. 5: 6, 7, 14)   (*NIV*)

SANCTIFIED AND BLAMELESS   261

May God himself,
     the God of peace,
   sanctify you through and through.
May your whole spirit, soul and body
   be kept blameless
     at the coming of our Lord Jesus Christ.
The one who calls you is faithful
   and he will do it.

(1 Thess. 5: 23–4)   *(NIV)*

THE GIFT OF PEACE BY THE LORD OF PEACE   262

Now may the Lord of peace himself
   give you peace
     at all times
     and in every way.
The Lord be with all of you.

(2 Thess. 3: 16)   *(NIV)*

THE PEACE OF GOD   263

Rejoice in the Lord always. . . .
The Lord is near.
Do not be anxious about anything,
   but in everything,
     by prayer and petition,
     with thanksgiving,
   present your requests to God.
And the peace of God,
     which transcends all understanding,
   will guard your hearts and your minds in Christ Jesus.

(Phil. 4: 4–7)   *(NIV)*

VESTRY PRAYERS

264   BEFORE WORSHIP

Lord God, Holy Spirit,
    touch now our offering of worship;
      by your grace may it glorify you
        and so bless us, your people.
Let there be healing,
    encouragement, cheer, and truth,
      in Christ's name.

Jamie Wallace

265   BEFORE WORSHIP

Heavenly Father,
    accept our worship,
    forgive our sins,
    bless the people we pray for,
    and bless us too,
      for Jesus' sake.

Jamie Wallace

266   AFTER SERVICE

As we have been hearers of your word today,
    give us grace, Lord, to be doers of it through this week,
      for Christ's sake.

(Jas. 1: 22)   *J. C.*

267   AFTER SERVICE

You are worthy, our Lord and God,
    to receive glory and honour and power,
    for you created all things,
      and by your will
        they were created and have their being.

(Rev. 4: 11)   *(NIV)*

BEFORE HOLY COMMUNION 268

Draw near to us now, O God,
      in the reading and preaching of your word;
By your Holy Spirit
      help us in the ministry of prayer;
Grant us your peace,
      to have and to share;
And when, in obedience to your Son's command,
      we break bread together,
          sustain us with his life.

Jamie Wallace

AFTER HOLY COMMUNION 269

Graciously accept, O God, this our eucharist, the sacrifice of praise and thanksgiving, and fill our hearts with the joy of your salvation, now and always.

Frank Colquhoun

AFTER HOLY COMMUNION 270

Worthy is the Lamb, who was slain,
      to receive power and wealth and wisdom and strength
          and honour and glory and praise!

(Rev. 5: 12)   *(NIV)*

THE CHURCH AT WORK

RENEWED FOR MISSION 271

Almighty God, who in the fellowship of this parish has given us a neighbourhood to serve and has entrusted us with the gospel of light, the sacraments of life, and the service of love:

Renew us with your Spirit, that in worship and in work we may be true to our profession as the mission of Christ in this world; in the strength and to the glory of his name.

C. B. Naylor

DEEPER PARISH LIFE 272

Almighty God, we pray for ourselves and for all who form the church of Jesus Christ in this place.

May your word be proclaimed and received among us, and the sacraments duly ministered.

Bless both clergy and laity, that we all may grow in the knowledge and love of Christ and may increase in effectiveness as his witnesses; by the power of the Spirit, and to your glory.

(Cf. Article XIX) *J. C.*

Almighty God, we pray that you will look in mercy on this
    our parish.
Among all who are baptized in Christ's name
        may there be no divisions that hinder us
        from being perfectly united in mind and thought.

                                            (1 Cor. 1: 10–17)

Where grief has been caused by anyone
        may we be ready to forgive and comfort.

                                            (2 Cor. 2: 5–8)

May the message proclaimed among us be that of Christ
    crucified,
        and may we heed it as the power and wisdom of God.

                                    (1 Cor. 2: 1–5 & 1: 23–4)

May our worship strengthen the church
        and bear witness that you are really among us.

                                            (1 Cor. 14: 24–6)

When we come together for the Lord's Supper,
        help us to examine our own selves
        and to proclaim his death until he comes.

                                            (1 Cor. 11: 26–8)

Deepen in us that overflowing joy
        which impels us to be generous in our offerings,
        but first to give our own selves to you.

                                            (2 Cor. 8: 2–5)

Fit us to be your ambassadors in the world,
        imploring men on Christ's behalf
        'Be reconciled to God'.

                                            (2 Cor. 5: 20)

Help us to stand firm in the faith,

                                            (1 Cor. 16: 13)

        to rejoice in our hope of glory,

                                            (2 Cor. 3: 11–12)

        and, above all, to have the love that never fails,

                                            (1 Cor. 13: 8 & 13)

        knowing the presence of the God of love and peace.

                                            (2 Cor. 13: 11)

                                            J. C.

FOLLOWING PARISH ELECTIONS   274

Our Lord and Master, we remember how in the early church many were called to be fellow-workers in Christ. Hear us now as we pray for those who have begun their terms of appointment as

> churchwardens,
> glebe wardens,
> members of the select vestry,
> †diocesan synodsmen, and
> †parochial nominators.

Help them to know your will in all the affairs of the church, to be guided by you in their duties, and gladly to devote their individual talents to your service here; so may we be a people united in serving you and witnessing to your name.

(Rom. 16: 3, 9)   J.C.

THE PARISH AT A TIME OF VACANCY

THE MAN GOD PREPARES   275

Shepherd of souls, give to us for the leadership of your
  church in this parish
> a man after your own heart,
> a man of faith and prayer, filled with the Spirit,
> a man of vision, wisdom, and sound judgment,
> a man with a pastoral heart and a true love for people.
Prepare the man of your choice for his ministry among us,
  and prepare us for his coming;
> and overrule in everything for
> > the doing of your will and
> > the furtherance of your glory;
> > > through Jesus Christ our Lord.

Frank Colquhoun

---

† This line will normally be used only after triennial elections.

276   A RENEWED CHURCH

Lord, call to this your church and ours
    a true shepherd,
    a man of God,
    a minister of Christ;
and make us, with him,
    a church joyful in worship,
        united in witness,
        working,
        caring,
        praising,
        loving,
      to the glory of your name;
        through Jesus Christ our Lord.

Timothy Dudley-Smith

277   THE BOARD OF NOMINATION

Lord Jesus, whom we love and acknowledge as Head of
    the church,
    we pray for all those who form the Board of Nomination
        for this parish;
      for our bishop,
      for our parochial nominators, and
      for the diocesan nominators.
May each have opportunity for quietness
      to meditate in God's word,
      to grow in your love, and
      to pray for the Holy Spirit's guidance.
Give each one grace to perform his or her duty
      in singleness of heart,
      for the glory of God,
      for the good of his church, and
      for the welfare of his people.
May they all be brought to that knowledge of your will
    which they will share
        with one another, and also
        with the one is to be called to this parish,
          as pastor of the flock
            for whom you gave yourself and rose again.

J. C.

The third section of petitions is derived from
chapter 4 of the Constitution of the Church of Ireland

THE DIOCESE

LINKED TO EACH OTHER, LED BY THE SPIRIT

Eternal Lord, we thank you for your mercy
 by which we can be known as God's church
  in this place.
May we, and all your people throughout this diocese of . . .,
 receive with joy and in full measure
  the grace and peace that come
   from God our Father
   and from the Lord Jesus Christ.
May we, and all our parishes, grow and be strengthened
 in loyalty to our Saviour and to each other,
 in love and unity with all others
  who profess his great name, and
 in our testimony, by our lives and by our words,
  to those who do not yet follow him.
Grant the whole fruit of the Spirit
 to N., our bishop;
 to all our clergy, and their families;
 to diocesan and general synodsmen;
 to members of councils, boards, and committees; and
 to all who share in the work of the parishes.
May the gifts exercised by each
  be the work of one and the same Spirit,
   to your glory.

(2 Cor. 1: 1–2; Gal. 5: 22; 1 Cor. 12: 4–11)   *J. C.*

279 A DIOCESAN BISHOP

Almighty God, we pray for your servant *N.*,
  bishop of this diocese.
Grant him your daily help,
    that he may be to us
        a wise and discerning leader,
        a caring and understanding pastor,
        a learned and faithful teacher.
May he have good health,
        safety in travelling,
    and, with all his family,
        the blessing of your presence in his home;
                                          for Christ's sake.

J. C.

280 FOR PAROCHIAL USE, FOLLOWING THE ELECTION OF
DIOCESAN SYNODSMEN, OR BEFORE SYNOD

Lord Jesus, Head of the church, we commend to you those who have been chosen from this parish to serve you as members of our diocesan synod.

Enable them faithfully to represent us to the diocese, and fairly to interpret the decisions of synod to us in the parish.

At the same time, enable them also to form their own views and take their own decisions, while always submitting themselves to what you teach them from your word and by the guidance of the Holy Spirit.

Strengthen them, we pray, in the face of every circumstance which could rob them of the time they need both to study the papers that are given them and in prayer to seek your will concerning the business of synod.

Help them to seek above all the glory of your name and the good of your church.

So we ask you to grant that as a result of their work and of that of the whole synod we, like the church at Antioch, may be gladdened and encouraged, to the praise of God the Father.

(Acts 15: 31)   *J. C.*

THE DIOCESE AT A TIME OF VACANCY

THE EPISCOPAL ELECTORAL COLLEGE 281

Almighty God, we pray for those on whom falls
    the responsibility for the election of a bishop
    for this diocese.
By the grace of the Holy Spirit,
    may they be prepared in heart and mind for their duties;
    may they in sincerity seek your guidance
        and in faith follow it;
    may they at all times act
        in singleness of heart,
        for your glory,
        for the good of your church, and
        for the welfare of your people.
Grant that the man of your choosing shall be appointed
    and shall be assured of your call.
Give him your help
    as he relinquishes his present work,
    moves home,
    and takes up his new task.
May he and all your people in the diocese
    be shown your ways
    and taught in your paths,
        in the name of Christ.

J. C.

The second petition contains allusions to chapter 6 of the
Constitution of the Church of Ireland.

A SYNOD

282   FOR A MEETING OF SYNOD

Heavenly Father, it is your purpose
    that there should be no division in the body and
    that its parts should have equal concern for each other.
We pray for members of the body of Christ
    meeting together in synod;
        grant to those who are timorous
           or unfamiliar with its procedures
                the sense that they belong, and can contribute to it;
        grant to those in positions of leadership
           the awareness that all its members
                are equal before you, and
           the ability to help and encourage others.
In debates and in decisions, may all be
    led by your Spirit and
    motivated by the love of Christ,
                  for his sake.

(1 Cor. 12: 25)   *J. C.*

283   BEFORE A MEETING OF SYNOD

Gracious God, we pray for the meeting of the . . . *Synod
    of this church.
May its members be drawn together in harmony of purpose
    and in dependence upon the Holy Spirit for guidance.
Help them in their debates to listen for what you are saying,
    and in their decisions to be brought in unity
        to the mind of Christ;
            in whose name we ask.

(1 Cor. 2: 16)   *J. C.*

* Here may be inserted the word 'General', or the word 'Diocesan'
prefixed by the name of the diocese.

THE ANGLICAN COMMUNION

PARTICULARLY FOR A TIME OF CONFERENCE   284

PARTNERS IN MISSION   284

Almighty God, you have called the churches of the Anglican communion to witness and service, and have richly blessed them.

Grant that the members of this world-wide family may plan and work together in brotherly love to further your mission to the world.

Remembering that the church which lives to itself will die by itself, may we receive humbly, give generously, and share joyfully the spiritual treasures and material resources you have entrusted to us; through our Lord and Saviour Jesus Christ.

John Kingsnorth

CYCLES.

PARTICULARLY FOR A TIME OF CONFERENCE   285

We give our thanks to you, almighty God,
   that you sent our Lord Jesus
      to be the Saviour of the world;
   that he has sent his servants
      to make disciples of all nations,
         baptizing them in the name of
            Father, Son and Holy Spirit; and
   that you have sent the same Holy Spirit
      into the hearts of the redeemed
         that they may together call upon you as Father.
We ask that we, with all bishops, clergy, and laity
      who are joined with us in the fellowship
         of the Anglican communion
   may be kept mindful that it is
      by your grace that we have been called;
      by your word that we are to be taught and trained; and
      by your Spirit that we can be enabled
         to witness to the nations,
            and guided to minister to the needy today.
May we be helped to remember our leaders' responsibilities
      and our own duty to pray for them
      and for all your church
         (especially on the occasion of . . .).
So may you be glorified in the church, the body of Christ.

(1 John 4: 14; Matt. 28: 19; Gal. 4: 6)   *J. C.*

CHRISTIAN UNITY

286   THE UNITY WE HAVE

We give thanks, our Father, for the unity
    which is already ours as Christians.
We thank you that there is
    one Body and one Spirit,
    one hope which belongs to our calling,
    one Lord, one faith, one baptism,
    one God and Father of us all.
And we resolve that by your grace
    we will live a life worthy of our calling, and
      be humble, gentle, and patient,
    bearing with one another in love, and
      keeping the unity of the Spirit
        through the bond of peace,
          for the sake of Jesus Christ our Lord.

(Eph. 4: 1–6)   *Frank Colquhoun*

287   'THAT THE WORLD MAY BELIEVE'

    Lord Jesus Christ, who prayed for your disciples that they
may be one, even as you are one with the Father; draw us to
yourself, that in common love and obedience to you we may be
united to one another, in the fellowship of the one Spirit, that the
world may believe that you are Lord, to the glory of God the
Father.

(John 17: 21)   *William Temple*

288   THE HINDRANCES IN US

Deliver us, Lord, from thinking so much
    about the differences between
    the individual parts of the body of Christ
      that we fail to fulfil your intention
      that we should be one body.
Deliver us, Lord, from taking such pride
    in the varying backgrounds from which we come
      that we fail to realize that all are sons of God
        through faith in Christ Jesus.

Deliver us, Lord, from such unbelief and impurity
 that we fail to be among the heavenly multitude
  from every nation, tribe, people, and language
   who cry out 'Salvation belongs to our God,
    who sits on the throne,
    and to the Lamb'.

(1 Cor. 12: 7–12; Gal. 3: 26–8; Rev. 21: 8, 27 & 7: 9–10)   *J. C.*

THE WORLD COUNCIL OF CHURCHES   289

 Almighty God, our heavenly Father, whose Son Jesus
Christ has broken down the barriers that divide people and races:
we ask you to bless the World Council of Churches, that it may
bear true witness to your activity in our midst, give voice to the
Christian concern for justice and holiness, and serve the needs of
the poor and under-privileged; and hasten the time, O God,
when your Church shall be one and be seen to be one; through the
same Jesus Christ our Lord.

(Eph. 2: 14)   *John Kingsnorth*

THE CHURCHES IN IRELAND   290

Father almighty, from whom the whole family
 in heaven and on earth derives its name:
We pray that out of your glorious riches
 you will so strengthen us and all the churches in Ireland
  that we all may be rooted and established in love;
  that Christ may dwell in our midst through faith;
  and
  that we may never boast in anything
   except his cross of Calvary.
Teach us to think less of those things
 which result from the work of men
 than of what you alone can bring to pass
  as a new creation.
So may peace and mercy be our rule,
 and the grace of our Lord Jesus Christ
  be with all who are brothers in him.

(Eph. 3: 15–17; Gal. 6: 14–18)   +SISTERS   *J. C.*

ORDINATION

291   PRAYING FOR LABOURERS

O God, you have told us to pray
     for more labourers in your harvest-field.
We ask you then
     to call many of your children
         to the work of the ministry, and
     to enable them by your grace
         to hear and act upon your call.
Make them at all times sensitive to your guidance,
                willing to learn, and
                   eager to serve.
We ask this in the name of him who came
     not to be ministered to but to minister,
     Jesus Christ, your Son, our Lord.

A. C. C. M.

292   VOCATION

Lord God, as we praise you for all the people in the Bible whom you called to serve you, we remember how some doubted—not the reality of their calling, but their own ability to fulfil it.

As we ask you now to call men and women to your service, we pray that you will assure them of your own unlimited resources available to all who obey you. Teach us to be supportive of them in fellowship, in prayer, and in giving.

So may your church be built up, to the glory of your name.

(Ex. 3: 11; 1 Sam. 10: 21–2; Jer. 1: 6)   *J. C.*

293   THOSE IN TRAINING

Lord of the harvest, we pray for those training to become
     pastors and teachers in your church.
Give them a deepening assurance of your call,
         an increasing experience of your life-giving Spirit,
         a strong conviction of revealed truth, and
         a holy boldness to make it known;

That they may equip your people for work in your service,
    and build up the body of Christ in faith and knowledge,
    to the glory of your great name.

(Eph. 4: 12–13)   *Michael Botting*

DEVELOPING OF CHRISTIAN CHARACTER   **294**

Grant, Lord, to those now called to ministry and service
    an increasing knowledge of the living God,
    confidence in the gospel and the Word of Life,
    compassion for the lost and needy,
    courage,
    endurance and
    unfailing love;
for Jesus' sake.

Timothy Dudley-Smith

FOR EMBER DAYS   **295**

Almighty God, who led your apostles to ordain ministers to
serve in all the churches: pour out your Holy Spirit on those who
are to be set apart at this time for the ministry of Word and
Sacrament; that they may be strengthened for the work to which
you have called them and be faithful shepherds of your flock, to
the glory of your name, through Jesus Christ our Lord.

(Acts 14: 23)   *Frank Colquhoun*

CLERGY

296   BISHOPS, PRIESTS, AND DEACONS

O God, you have chosen men to serve you
    in the ministry of your church,
    and have given them a perfect example
    in the person of your Son Jesus Christ.
We ask your blessing on all bishops, priests, and deacons
    (especially . . .).
Let them never forget the privilege of their calling,
    nor shirk its responsibilities.
Keep them in your love, that they may be
    good shepherds of your people and
    true servants of him who is our great High Priest,
                    Jesus Christ our Lord.

A. C. C. M.

297   THE MINISTRY AMONG PEOPLE

Lord Jesus Christ, Apostle, Priest, and Servant, bless the
bishops, priests, and deacons of your church; may they lead your
people boldly, walk with them lovingly, and send them forth
joyfully to proclaim the good news of your kingdom where you
live for ever and ever.

A. C. C. M.

298   THE INCUMBENT OF THE PARISH

Almighty Father, lover of mankind and
    giver of all that is good:
    hear our prayers for your servant
        whom you have called to the charge of this parish.
Strengthen him, O Lord, by your Holy Spirit and
    fill him with love for your people;
    that as a faithful priest
    and true servant of your Son
    he may preach your word,
        minister your sacraments, and
        shepherd your flock,
            to the glory of your name;
            through Jesus Christ our Lord.

Frank Colquhoun

THE APOSTOLIC CHARGE 299

Lord of the church, we pray for all those who have been
  called to ministry in your church.
Like those who were called in apostolic times,
    may they not hesitate to proclaim the whole will of God,
      remembering their duty to guard their own selves;
    may they be concerned to guard all the flock,
      remembering that the Holy Spirit
        has made them overseers;
    may they be faithful as shepherds of your church,
      remembering that Christ has bought it
        with his own blood;
    may they be enabled to give themselves in hard work,
      remembering the words of the Lord Jesus
        'It is more blessed to give than to receive'.
Following the example of the apostle Paul,
    we commit them to God and to the word of his grace,
      which can build them up
      and give them an inheritance among the sanctified,
        where all shall praise your name for ever.

(Acts 20: 26–35)   *J. C.*

THE PASTORAL MINISTRY 300

Pour out your Holy Spirit, O Lord, on all
    whom you have called to serve your church
      as pastors and teachers.
Give them wise and understanding hearts;
fill them with a true love for your people;
make them holy, and
keep them humble;
    that they may be faithful shepherds,
      feeding the flock committed to their care,
      and ever seeking
        your glory and
        the increase of your kingdom;
          through Jesus Christ our Lord.

(Ezek. 34: 1–8)   *Frank Colquhoun*

301   THE PASTOR'S OWN NEEDS

Grant, Lord God, to those whom you have called
    to be shepherds of your people
  that they may be patient listeners
    to those who bring them their burdens,
      trustworthy recipients of their confidences,
      ready discerners of their true points of need,
      wise advisors to those who look for guidance,
      practical helpers to those who cannot cope alone,
        and in all they do
    faithful ministers of Jesus Christ,
      the great Shepherd of the sheep.
In all the burdens and sorrows
        which they are called upon to share
  may they themselves be kept
      from faltering or stumbling,
    through daily strengthening from your word, and
    through the gracious working of your Holy Spirit.

(Col. 1: 7; Heb. 13: 20; 1 Pet. 5: 20)   *J. C.*

302   GIVING OUT AND TAKING IN

Almighty God, give to all whom you have called to the
sacred ministry of your church such a sense of their high calling
that they may reckon no self-sacrifice too great for them to make
in your service.

Grant that while ministering your blessings to their people
they may continually be filled with your blessing upon themselves; for the sake of Jesus Christ our Lord.

Canon Peter Green

303   SELECTION AND TRAINING FOR THE MINISTRY

God our Father, by the power of your Spirit you call and
equip your people for the work of ministry in the Body of your
Son; guide those who have the responsibility of discerning where
you would have each of us serve you; and bless the work of those
who, through their teaching and example, prepare men and
women for ministry, that the church may be strengthened and
your kingdom enlarged. We ask this in the name of Jesus Christ
our Lord.

David Silk

PASTORAL AND DEVOTIONAL

ADDICTION

DELIVERANCE IN CHRIST 304

We rejoice, heavenly Father, in the promise that in your Son
Jesus Christ there is perfect freedom.

In his name we pray for those who are subject to the slavery
of sin, by gambling and betting, by excessive drinking, by
addiction to drugs, and by the misuse of their sexual instincts.

Enable them by the power of your Spirit to overcome these
evil compulsions, and in your mercy grant them the liberty you
offer them in abundance through Jesus Christ our Lord.

Michael Botting

ALCOHOLICS 305

Gracious Lord, who has given to men
    so many good things that by sin we can defile:
We pray for those now enslaved by alcoholism;
As we ask for their deliverance from its grip,
                        its degradation,
                and its sin,
    we praise you for the power of Jesus the Saviour
      to set men free.
Teach us how dependent we ourselves are
          on his grace day by day,
      how responsible we are
          for not causing other men to stumble, and
      how wonderful is the message that
          if anyone is in Christ he is a new creation.

(1 Cor. 10: 32; 2 Cor. 5: 17)   *J. C.*

306 DRUG ADDICTS

Lord Jesus Christ, you have promised perfect liberty
    to those who trust you:
We cry to you for those who are at this moment
    enslaved by their own need of drugs;
Raise up men and women with the skills to assist them,
    and give them the care they need;
Turn back those young people who have already begun
    the drift towards addiction;
Help us to see how we may bear one another's burdens;
And, for those for whom treatment has come too late,
        grant your mercy,
            the awareness of sin,
            the awareness of yourself, and
            peace at the last,
    for your holy name's sake.

(John 8: 36)   *C. Idle*

ADVANCING YEARS

307 UNTIL THE SHADOWS LENGTHEN

Support us, O Lord, all the day long of this troubled life,
    until the shadows lengthen,
    and the evening comes,
    and the busy world is hushed,
    the fever of life is over,
    and our work is done.
Then Lord, in your mercy, grant us
    a safe lodging,
    a holy rest, and
    peace at the last;
        through Jesus Christ our Lord.

Ascribed to John Henry Newman

ASSURANCE IN CHRIST   **308**

Lord Jesus, we remember that it was the elderly who had the perception to recognize you when you first appeared in the temple, and for whom your coming was the assurance of peace and redemption.

Reveal yourself now, we pray, to those among our community who are old and may be burdened and weary; grant them assurance of peace and redemption, by your mercy and grace.

(Luke 2: 25–38)   *J. C.*

THOSE IN RESIDENTIAL CARE   **309**

Look with mercy, O God our Father, on those whose increasing years bring them weakness, distress, or isolation.

Provide for them homes of dignity and peace; give them understanding helpers, and the willingness to accept help; and, as their strength diminishes, increase their faith and their assurance of your love.

This we ask in the name of Jesus Christ our Lord.

Episcopal Church, USA

NEARING THE END OF THE ROAD   **310**

We lovingly commend to you, Lord Jesus,
   those in our parish who can now look back
      through the memories of almost a life-time.
Gladden their hearts
   with the recollection of joys and blessings, and
   with thankfulness for family and friends.
Above all, give them the peace, assurance, and serenity
   of knowing your pardon and cleansing
      for all that has been wrong in past times;
   your comfort and provision for these days, and
   your promise of a place for evermore
      in your Father's house,
         that they may be with you where you are,
         in heavenly glory.

(John 14: 2–3)   *J. C.*

ART

311   ARTISTS AND CRAFTSMEN

O God, whose spirit in our hearts teaches us
    to desire your perfection,
    to seek for truth, and
    to rejoice in beauty:
Enlighten and inspire all artists and craftsmen
    in whatever is true, pure, and lovely,
      that your name may be honoured and
        your will done on earth;
            for Jesus' sake.

Society of St Luke the Painter

312   APPRECIATION OF ART

We thank you, God of creation,
      for the faculties by which we may perceive beauty
      and for the heart with which to love it.
Give us eyes to see and ears to hear
      each sight and sound which tells of your love for man.
Since you are far greater than the works of your own hands,
      let us not be content to love your world
        without much more loving you
          through Jesus Christ, who is before all things
          and in whom all things hold together.

(Col. 1: 17)   *Dick Williams*

BEREAVEMENT

WHO SHALL SEPARATE? 313

God of hope and giver of all comfort, we commend to your keeping those who mourn the loss of loved ones (and especially those for whom we have been asked to pray).

Give them the peace that passes all understanding, and make them to know that neither death nor life can separate them from your love in Jesus Christ our Lord.

(Phil. 4: 7; Rom. 8: 35–9) *Frank Colquhoun*

THE ENTRY TO A BRIGHTER AND FULLER LIFE 314

O Lord, we ask you to comfort all who mourn
the death of those whom they love.
May they be
uplifted by the memory of their affection and example;
strengthened by your continual presence and power;
encouraged by the knowledge that
for those who love you
death is not a precipice over which we fall,
to be seen no more,
but a horizon beyond which we pass
into a brighter and fuller life;
through Jesus Christ our Lord.

John Eddison

OUT OF DARKNESS INTO LIGHT 315

Eternal Father, by whose mighty power our Lord Jesus
has been raised from the dead:
Strengthen by your Holy Spirit all those who mourn.
Lead them to worship you
with reverent and submissive hearts.
Help them to put their whole trust
in your perfect wisdom, power, and love.
Bless them in reading the words of Scripture,
that by them they may find hope
and be lifted above darkness and distress
into the light and peace of your presence,
through Jesus Christ our living Lord.

Adapted from Orders and Prayers for Church Worship

316   LONELINESS

Father of compassion, and God of all comfort,
    we commend to you those
            who fear the silence of a home now lonely and
            who grieve at the empty chair.
Be especially close to them now.
Send the Holy Spirit to make your presence real to them.
Help them to find hope from your word.
Show us how, in love, we may comfort them
    and obey your command
        to look after them in their distress;
              in Christ's name.

(2 Cor. 1: 3–4; Jas. 1: 27)   *J. C.*

317   THE DAYS AHEAD

Grant, O Lord, to all who are bereaved the spirit of faith and
courage, that they may have strength to meet the days to come
with steadfastness and patience; not sorrowing as those without
hope, but in thankful remembrance of your great goodness in
past years, and in the sure expectation of a joyful reunion in
heaven; and this we ask in the name of Jesus Christ our Saviour.

Episcopal Church, USA

318   THE LOSS OF A CHILD

Loving God, the healer of broken hearts:
Look down in tender pity and compassion
        on your servants whose joy has been turned
           to mourning.
Do not leave them in their sadness,
    but grant that by their common sorrow
        they may be drawn closer to you
        and to one another.
Fill their souls with the light and the comfort
    of your presence.
Bless their home with your love and peace.
At all times, uphold them with your power and
        guide them by your Spirit.
So may their family be united in heaven,
        through Jesus Christ our Lord.

Adapted from Orders & Prayers for Church Worship

CHILDREN

THE BIRTH OF A BABY   319

Heavenly Father, creator and giver of life, there is much joy in our hearts at the news of a baby's birth—a most special and complete gift of your love, a new being and a wonder of creation.

Be with the mother and father of this little baby in their happiness, and accept their praise and ours as we give thanks to you through Jesus Christ our Lord.

Mothers' Union Prayer Book

TRANSMITTING OUR FAITH   320

Dear Father, we give you thanks for children, and particularly for those who are committed to our care. We thank you for their innocent ways, for their laughter, for their love, and for their unquestioning trust in us.

By what we tell them and by what we do, help us Father to give them a simple and steadfast faith, a loving heart and a cheerful disposition, that they may be equipped to be citizens not only of this world but also of the next, through Jesus Christ our Lord.

Patricia Mitchell

321   PRAISE FOR CHILDREN

Lord Jesus, who delighted to take little children in your arms
                    and bless them:
hear us as we declare to you
            our love for babies and children,
            our joy at the wonder of their creation,
            our fascination at seeing them grow and develop,
            our longing that they may walk with you
                    through life,
            our thanks for every happy memory of them.
We confess that there are those times when
        we get annoyed by them and weary of coping with them.
Forgive us when we sin against them, and grant
        that they may suffer no lasting harm because of us, and
        that we and they together may live and grow in grace,
            each learning from the other and from you,
            and increasing in the knowledge and love of God,
                our heavenly Father and Creator.

(Mark 10: 16)   *J. C.*

322   GROWING UP

Heavenly Father, we pray for our children in their life at
        home and at school.
Watch over them and protect them from evil;
        guide them into the ways of your will; and
        prepare them for the work to which you are calling
            them in the life of the world;
            for the sake of Jesus Christ our Lord.

                                        Llewellyn Cumings

323   HANDICAPPED CHILDREN

God our Father, we commend to your compassion
        all children who are in need;
            those whose bodies are handicapped by injury or illness;
            those whose minds are retarded; and
            those whose lives are warped by broken marriages and
                unhappy homes.

Enable all who care for them
to minister with tenderness and understanding;
And give them the assurance of your unfailing love;
through Christ our Lord.

Frank Colquhoun

THOSE WHO HAVE LOST PARENTS 324

Almighty God, we thank you for teaching us about your fatherly care through your Son Jesus, and trusting in it we commend to your loving kindness all children who have lost their parents.

Give special inspiration and grace to those who look after them in the early moments of their bereavement. Give great love and joy to those who care for them over the following years.

In and through their bereavement help these children to trust you as their heavenly Father, knowing that their earthly parents are in your care; grant that they may come to the maturity that rests in confidence in you, the helper and defender of the fatherless.

(Ps. 10: 14, 18) *Dick Williams*

THOSE WHO HAVE BEEN SINNED AGAINST 325

O God, whose Son Jesus Christ took the children into his arms and blessed them: hear our prayer for those children who are suffering through the sin, cruelty, and stupidity of men and women.

Wipe out from their souls the stain and misery of fear, and give back to them the trustfulness and untroubled joy that should be theirs.

To those who look after them and teach them grant faith that you are able to do this, and patient wisdom to co-operate with you; for the sake of Jesus Christ our Lord.

(Mark 10: 16) *Frank Colquhoun*

CHRISTIAN EDUCATION

326   JESUS' LOVE AND EXAMPLE

Lord Jesus, we thank and praise you that in your earthly life
    you were glad to have children brought to you,
    you prayed for them, and
    you gave them your blessing.
We need your help in the great task of bringing up
    the boys and girls for whom we are responsible.
We ask that we ourselves may be taught
    by our heavenly Father,
    looking humbly to him as his children.
May we be delivered
    from causing any harm to boys and girls,
    in body, mind, or spirit.
Instead, may we love them,
    and welcome them to share with us in your
    kingdom, rejoicing together in your glory.

(Matt. 19: 13–15 & 18: 3–6)   *J. C.*

327   OUR RESPONSIBILITY

Lord, guard our children
    in the temptations that surround them,
    and help us to give them the right values;
    help us to impress upon them
    that you have standards of right and wrong;
    help us to show them the importance of truth;
    help us to teach them the meaning of real love;
    help us to be honest about our own shortcomings;
    help us to introduce them to the only one
    who can be with them at all times,
    Jesus Christ our Lord.

Beryl Bye

328   CHILDREN IN SUNDAY SCHOOL

Father, we pray for the children of our Sunday School:
    help them to know you as their heavenly Father;
    make them aware of the reality of your love
    in the person of Jesus;

help them by your Holy Spirit to learn
to love you and to work for you;
give them courage to be true to you and to themselves,
with other people, and at school.
Be with each one, and bless all,
that they may be joyful members of your family;
through Jesus Christ our Lord.

Patricia Mitchell

SUNDAY SCHOOL TEACHERS 329

Almighty Father, the only wise God,
source of all grace and truth:
enlighten the minds of those who teach the young
in this parish;
give them understanding of their task, and
a true love for those they serve;
help them both in their lives and by their teaching
to set forward the cause of true religion
and sound learning;
through Jesus Christ our Lord.

Frank Colquhoun

COMMITMENT AND CONSECRATION

330   KNOWLEDGE, LOVE, AND SERVICE OF GOD

Eternal God, the light of the minds that know you,
    the joy of the hearts that love you, and
    the strength of the wills that serve you:
Grant us so to know you that we may truly love you, and
    so to love you that we may fully serve you,
    whom to serve is perfect freedom,
        in Jesus Christ our Lord.

After St Augustine

331   SURRENDERED TO GOD AND PROTECTED BY HIM

Almighty Lord and everlasting God,
    we acknowledge our need of your rule
    in our hearts and in our bodies;
        that in our hearts there may grow
        the knowledge of your laws, and
        that our bodies may be set apart
        for living according to them.
Through your most mighty protection,
    both now and always,
    may we be preserved in body and soul
        by our Lord and Saviour Jesus Christ.

Adapted from Book of Common Prayer

332   BEING SEEN TO BE THE PEOPLE OF GOD

As God's chosen people, holy and dearly loved,
    may we clothe ourselves with compassion,
                kindness,
                humility,
                gentleness, and
                patience;
    may we bear with each other
        and forgive whatever grievances we may have
        against one another—
        forgiving as the Lord forgave us;
    and over all these virtues may we put on love,
        for we ask it all in Christ's name.

(Col. 3: 12–14)   *J. C.*

UNWAVERING DEDICATION   **333**

Grant, Lord, that we may
   hold to you without parting,
   worship you without wearying,
   serve you without failing;
     faithfully seek you,
     happily find you, and
     for ever possess you,
       the only God, blessed now and for ever.

St Anselm

TAKE US AND KEEP US   **334**

Use me, my Saviour, for whatever purpose,
   and in whatever way you require.
Here is my poor and empty heart;
   fill it with your grace.
Here is my sinful and troubled soul;
   give it new life with your love.
Take my heart and live in it;
take my mouth to declare the glory of your name;
take my love and all my powers to advance your kingdom.
Relying wholly on your grace,
   may all your church be built up in the faith
   and kept from falling,
     till you present it
       before the Father's glorious presence
         without fault and with great joy,
         to your glory for evermore.

(Jude 24–5)   *Dwight L. Moody*

GOD'S FULL COMMAND OF THE FULLY SURRENDERED   **335**

Take command, O Lord, of the citadel of our hearts,
   and reach out into every corner of our lives.
Make us strong to resist evil,
   quick to learn your way,
   ready to do your will.
Help us to love you with all our hearts,
   and to show our love not only with our lips,
     but in our lives,
       by giving up ourselves to your service, and
       by walking before you in holiness and righteousness
         all our days,
           through Jesus Christ our Lord.

John Eddison

336   HEARING THE WORD AND BEARING FRUIT

Grant, Almighty God, that the words which we have heard today with our ears may by your grace be so grafted in our hearts that they may bring forth in us the fruit of good living, to the honour and praise of your name; through Jesus Christ our Lord.

Adapted from Book of Common Prayer

337   HUMILITY

O Lord Jesus Christ, for our sakes
    you left the light and glory of your father's presence;
    you came and lived among us in poverty, and
    you suffered shame and death on the cross.
Give us a determination like yours,
    that we may not seek great things for ourselves,
    but may follow in the steps of your way of humility,
                for your name's sake.

John Eddison

338   COURAGE

O Lord Jesus Christ, you inspired your followers with such courage that in your name they resisted temptation, overcame opposition, and attempted things which seemed impossible.

Give us, we pray, the same courage, that we may choose the hard right instead of the easy wrong, not minding what other people think or say, or whether they laugh.

When we are tempted to waver, may we remember the courage with which you endured the cross and thought nothing of the shame, because of the joy you had in doing your Father's will.

We ask this for your name's sake.

(Heb. 12: 2)   *John Eddison*

THE TONGUE   **339**

Set a guard, Lord, upon our tongues, that we may never speak the cruel word which is not true; or being true is not the whole truth; or being wholly true is merciless, for the love of Jesus Christ our Lord.

(Ps. 34: 13; Jas. 1: 26)   *Daily Prayer*

THE DEPARTED

THE COMMUNION OF SAINTS   **340**

We give thanks to you, our Father,
    for all your servants departed this life in your faith and
      fear;
    for the memory of their words and deeds;
    for the sure and certain hope of reunion with them
      hereafter;
    for the joy that is now theirs, free from earth's sin and
      sorrow; and
    for our communion with them in your Son, Jesus Christ
      our Lord.

Frank Colquhoun

PRAISE IN HEAVEN AND EARTH   **341**

God of the living and Father of our risen Lord:
    we are glad in your presence today
    as we remember those who have gone before us
      believing your promises and
      trusting in your mercy.
Help us to follow them as they followed Christ,
    and with all your people on earth and in heaven
    to give you the glory and the praise that is your due;
      through Jesus Christ our Lord.

C. Idle

THE DISADVANTAGED

342   OUR OWN RESPONSIBILITY

O God of love, who has always required
        that man should be just:
Forgive us for our complacency,
                for our lack of care for others,
                for thinking that the welfare state relieves us of
                responsibility for them,
                for thinking that all is well with the poor, the
                hungry, and the handicapped.
Open our eyes to injustices around us,
        and help us to give up
                ourselves,
                our time,
                our comfort, and
                our possessions
        in the service of Jesus Christ and
                of those for whom he came to bring life to the full.

Susan Williams

343   THE HANDICAPPED

O God, the Father of the helpless, we pray for handicapped
people and all who suffer from any kind of disability.

Give them fresh courage to face each day, and the comfort of
the knowledge that you love and care for them.

Open our eyes and touch our hearts, that we may be
sensitive to their needs and do all that we can to help them, for
Jesus Christ's sake.

Mothers' Union Prayer Book

344   THE BLIND, THE DUMB, THE DEAF, AND THE LAME

Gracious and almighty God, we thank you for your promise
        by the prophet Isaiah that
                the eyes of the blind would be opened,
                the ears of the deaf unstopped,
                the tongue of the dumb shout for joy,
        and that the lame would leap like a deer.

We praise you for the fulfilment of that promise
   in your Son Jesus Christ
   and through his disciples.
May those who today suffer from handicap
   experience his power and grace
      in their bodily frailties and
      in their spiritual needs,
   through him who healed all who had need of healing,
       our Lord Jesus Christ.

(Isa. 35: 5–6; Luke 9: 11)   *J. C.*

THE DISTRESSED   **345**

God, whose mercy and compassion never fail:
Look kindly upon the sufferings of all mankind;
   the needs of the homeless,
   the anxieties of prisoners;
   the pains of the sick and the injured,
   the sorrows of the bereaved,
   the helplessness of the aged and weak.
Comfort and strengthen them for the sake of your Son,
   our Saviour Jesus Christ.

(Lam. 3: 22)   *St Anselm*

THE HUNGRY   **346**

God our Father, whose Son Jesus Christ looked with
compassion on the hungry people of his day and fed them: hear
us as we pray in his name for the starving and undernourished
peoples of our world.

Show us, who have so much, what we can do to help those
who have so little; and guide and prosper the efforts of those who
plan relief and are giving aid, that out of your bounty to mankind
the needs of all may be supplied.

Frank Colquhoun

347   REFUGEES AND OTHER HOMELESS PEOPLE

O God, the Father of our Lord Jesus Christ,
  who in perfect love for man
    chose to live as one who had nowhere
      to lay his head:
We pray for all who are homeless,
    all refugees,
      all who must live in exile or in a strange land;
Grant them human friendship in their need and loneliness,
    the chance of a new beginning,
      with the courage to take it,
        and, above all,
      an abiding faith in your sure love and care;
                      through Jesus Christ our Lord.

Christian Aid

348   THOSE WITHOUT HOME, WORK AND HOPE

Lord Jesus Christ, you were born in a stable,
    and had no home of your own on earth.
We ask you to bless every servant of yours who is working
    to give homes to the homeless,
      work to the workless, and
        hope to those who have lost hope,
    that they may all come to your everlasting home,
      where you reign with the Father and the Holy
        Spirit for ever.

(Luke 2: 7; 9: 58)   *C. M. Gray-Stack*

DISTRESS AND SUFFERING

349   THOSE IN PAIN

Merciful Father, help all who suffer pain of body, or grief of
heart, to find in you their help.

As Jesus suffered pain in his body, and healed it in others,
help them to find their peace in him, and to be renewed in
strength of body and mind; by your mercy.

Dick Williams

THE VALLEYS   350

Gracious God, we rejoice that you draw near in love
          to all who are in need.
We pray for all who are passing through
          the valley of weeping*;
     may it be to them a place of life-giving springs
     that shall strengthen them to appear before you.
For those who walk through
          the valley of the shadow of death we also pray;
     may they be delivered from fear of evil
     and comforted by your presence and your support,
          that they may dwell in your house for ever.

(Ps. 84: 6–7; Ps. 23)   *J. C.*

* Or 'dryness', as translated in the Liturgical Psalter.

THE INCURABLE   351

Father we bring to you the needs of those
          whose lives are shadowed by suffering,
     praying especially for those
          whose sickness has no cure,
          whose sadness finds no comfort, and
          whose loneliness can never be filled.
Bind up their wounds, O Lord,
     and lift their hearts to you,
as now in silence we remember them in Jesus' name.

                                              Frank Colquhoun

THE TERMINALLY ILL   352

     We thank you, our Father, that there is nothing in death or
life that can separate us from your love, and that whether we live
or die we belong to you.
     Give this confidence to your servant *N.*, whom we now
lovingly remember and commend to your mercy and care; and
grant him / her your peace to the journey's end—the peace that
passes all understanding in Christ Jesus our Lord.

(Rom. 8: 38–9)   *Frank Colquhoun*

353 *[handwritten: LORD]*   IN TIME OF DISASTER

[handwritten: AS WE JOIN IN THE PAIN + SUFFERING OF OUR AMERICAN BROTHERS/SISTERS]

~~Lord~~, we pray for all those whose homes
          have been darkened by disaster,
and also for those whose faith has been shaken;
         for those who stand bewildered and fearful in the
            midst of tragedy;
         for the injured, the bereaved, and the destitute.
We commend to your grace all who are seeking
      to help and heal the injured, and
      to comfort and calm the bereaved.
From you alone can come the word
         that will lift them above their darkness;
      answer, O Lord, the questions in men's minds,
      and assure them that, though disaster is not of your will,
      you are present with them in their suffering and sorrow,
      and can enable them to find purpose, hope, and peace
        again.

Stanley Pritchard

354   VICTIMS OF DISASTER AND RELIEF WORKERS

Lord of compassion and power:
      be with those who have survived this disaster,
      and minister to their needs of body, mind, and spirit.
Heal and help those who are injured;
      give peace to the dying;
      comfort and support the bereaved;
    to all who are working to bring relief and restore order,
      give strength and resilience to do their work well,
         through Jesus Christ our Lord.

Dick Williams

[handwritten list:]
RESCUERS......
FIREMEN ....
AMBULANCE ...
POLICE ...
ARMY ...
CITIZENS.
BLOOD DONORS

FAMILY NEEDS

WHEN A BIRTH IS EXPECTED 355

Creator God, the giver of all life,
  we pray for all mothers who await the birth of a child.
May they, like Samuel's mother, rejoice in you,
    and dedicate each new life to you.
We ask that from infancy these children
  may be brought up in families
      where there is a sincere faith in Jesus, and
      where the holy Scriptures are known;
May they grow into men and women of God,
    thoroughly equipped for every good work,
      to the glory of your name.

(1 Sam. 1: 26; 2 Tim. 1: 5 & 3: 14–15)   *J. C.*

TESTING TIMES IN THE FAMILY 356

Heavenly Father, bless the homes of our parish,
    especially those where to the joys of family life
      anxiety and sorrow have been added.
We cannot ask that we be spared
    from all difficulty and temptation;
    instead we ask that both parents and children
      may increase in the experience of your grace,
      may be strengthened in their faith, and
      may grow as your loyal servants,
                    through Christ the Lord.

J. C.

357   TIMES OF TENSION AND DIVISION

Father in heaven, pattern of all parenthood and lover of children, we pray for all homes and families where there is special need in times of bitterness, tension, or division. Give repentance to those who have failed, and willingness to forgive to those who have been wronged.

May parents and children together be learners in the school of Christ, daily increasing in mutual respect and understanding, with tolerance and patience, and in all-prevailing love; through Jesus Christ our Lord.

Timothy Dudley-Smith

358   ABSENT LOVED ONES

Almighty Father, you watch with love over all your children; mercifully hear our prayers for those whom we love and from whom we are now parted.

Be with them, Lord, and protect them in all the trials of this life. Teach us, and them, to feel and know that you are always near, and that we are never parted from each other if we are united in you through Jesus Christ our Lord.

Michael Buckley

359   SCATTERED FAMILIES

God of grace, to whose throne all who are in Christ have
      an access that knows no barriers of time or distance:
We bring before you in the fellowship of prayer and praise
      all members of our families now parted from us;
            be with them in their pleasures and in their joys,
            help them in sickness, danger, or difficulty,
            keep them and us in the love
                  of our Saviour Jesus Christ.

(Eph. 2: 18)   *J. C.*

HANDICAPPED CHILDREN   **360**

We pray Lord for families to whom has come a little one
  who is handicapped, crippled, or maimed;
  who seems unable to share fully
      in the daily life we take for granted;
  who calls for unceasing support and care
      from mother and father, brother and sister.
Give to all of them that strength of body and mind
      that shall enable them to cope
      with every unlooked-for burden.
Help them to respond to the child's great dependence on
  them with a calm and settled love
      that keeps them giving and caring
      and reflects a deeper realization of the love of Jesus,
          who called little children to himself, and
          who gave himself for us all.
Help us Lord to give ourselves
      to all who need our support and care,
              for Christ's sake.

J. C.

ONE-PARENT FAMILIES   **361**

Loving Father, we ask you to bless fathers and mothers who
are alone in bringing up their families.

Guide and strengthen them when they are beset by doubts
and difficulties; help them to lead their children to know and love
you; and assure them of your presence at all times; for Jesus
Christ's sake.

Mothers' Union Prayer Book

FRIENDS

DEEPENING FRIENDSHIPS   **362**

We commit into your protection, O Lord, our friends and
all who are dear to us. Make us always grateful for the happiness
and companionship which they bring into our lives. Help us
never to fail or disappoint them, but at all times may they be able
to count upon our loyalty and sympathy. Above all we ask you
that our friendships may be deepened and enriched through our
knowledge of the perfect friend, our Saviour Jesus Christ.

John Eddison

363   MOVING AWAY FROM THE PARISH

We thank you, Lord, for our years of fellowship
      with our friends who are leaving* this parish,
and pray that in their new neighbourhood they may find
      a ready welcome by the church,
      a door of opportunity in your service, and
      the peace of your presence.
Give them your help in practical matters like
      moving home,
      taking up a new job,
      making new friends, and
      settling into new schools.
Help us all to be faithful towards each other in prayer
      and to be increasingly thankful
            for the communion of saints,
                  through Christ our Lord.

* Or 'who have recently left'   *J. C.*

364   ABSENT FRIENDS

We thank you, gracious Lord, that modern communications make it so much less difficult for us to keep in touch with friends and members of the family who now live at a distance from us.

We thank you too that by the one Holy Spirit, and at any time, we can all have instant access to you, and be together in your presence.

As we rejoice in these privileges, we pray now for those whom we especially remember before you, asking that you will help them in their needs of the hour, and will keep them and us continually walking in your way until we all come together in your glory.

(Eph. 2: 18)   *J. C.*

THE FRIENDLESS **365**

Father, we bring to you in prayer
  people whose lives are starved of friendship;
  those who find it difficult to make friends;
  those who are cut off from friends by distance; and
  those who in old age have lost the friends they had.
Comfort and sustain them, O Lord, with your love.
Help them to discover new interests in life, and
  to seek fellowship in the family of the church.
Above all, may they find a friend in Jesus
  and daily enjoy his companionship.
We ask it for them in his name.

Frank Colquhoun

GUIDANCE

FOR A TIME OF UNCERTAINTY **366**

Lord, we look to you that in your mercy you will receive our prayers for your leading.

Help us to know your will and to be assured of your commands, and give us your grace and power to obey them; through Jesus Christ our Lord.

Adapted from Book of Common Prayer

'THEY WILL PRAY, . . . I WILL LEAD' **367**

O God, by whom the meek are guided in their judgments, and through whom the godly find light in times of darkness:

In all our doubts and uncertainties teach us to ask you for guidance, and save us by the wisdom of the Holy Spirit from every wrong choice.

In your light may we see light, and along your path may we not stumble; by the grace of Jesus Christ our Lord.

(Ps. 36: 9; Jer. 31: 9)   *William Bright*

HOLIDAYS

368 GOOD WEATHER, GOOD HEALTH, AND THEIR GIVER

We commend to you, O Lord, all those who at this time are seeking the rest and recreation of a holiday, and especially any who are known to us. Grant them, if it be your will, fine weather and freedom from accident or illness. And grant too that in their enjoyment they may not forget you, the giver of all good gifts, through Jesus Christ our Lord.

John Eddison

369 RECREATION OF BODY, MIND, AND SPIRIT

O God our Father, we thank you for the times of rest from the normal daily round. We pray that those who are on holiday at this time may be enabled to find the threefold recreation of body, mind, and spirit that will strengthen them for your service in the days that lie ahead; through Jesus Christ our Lord.

Bernard Woolf

370 SPIRITUAL STRENGTH AND BODILY REFRESHMENT

Lord Jesus, we remember how you needed to withdraw
    from the daily pressures of life in Galilee,
and so we pray today for your servants
    who are on holiday.
Like you, may they be strengthened by drawing near
        to God the Father;
    may they be refreshed by rest and relaxation;
    may they find happiness among family and
        friends;
    may they be prepared to meet and overcome
        whatever pressures shall confront them
            when they return to daily responsibilities;
    and, day by day,
        may we all live to your honour and glory.

(Luke 5: 16)   *J. C.*

HOME LIFE

HAPPINESS IS . . . 371

We thank you Lord for the security and happiness of home, for the love of parents and children, and for the companionship of relations and friends. May the love that unites us grow deeper with the years, and remain unspoiled by selfishness, ingratitude, or pride. May a thoughtful, generous spirit blossom amongst us, nourished by the love we have for you, and by our desire to please you in everything we do, through Jesus Christ our Lord.

John Eddison

BROKEN HOMES 372

O Lord Jesus Christ, Son of a virgin, born in a stable, and carried as a baby into exile: have mercy on all children who lack settled homes and dwelling-places, and grant that those whose families are divided by sin, or have been separated by law, may be united in the family of your church and brought at last to your heavenly home.

(Luke 2: 7; Matt. 2: 14) *C. M. Gray-Stack*

MARRIAGE

ENGAGED COUPLES 373

Lord Jesus Christ, who by your presence and power
      brought joy to the wedding at Cana:
Bless those engaged to be married, that there may be
    truth at the beginning of their lives together,
    unselfishness all the way, and
    perseverance to the end.
May their hopes be realized,
      and their love for each other deepen and grow,
        that through them your name may be glorified.

(John 2: 1–11) *Mothers' Union Service Book*

374   ENGAGED COUPLES

Thank you, Lord Jesus Christ, that you were present to
bless those at the wedding at Cana in Galilee.

We ask for your blessing now upon those engaged to be
married in accordance with your gracious purpose. Grant that
they may grow in honesty, maturity, and love for each other, and
that their married lives may draw their strength and unity from
you, and may reflect your glory to others.

(John 2: 1–11)   *C. Idle*

375   AS WEDDING DAY APPROACHES

We ask your blessing Lord on every engaged couple whose
wedding day approaches. During the last weeks before it, when
there is so much to occupy their time, grant them a deepening
conviction of their love for each other and of your call to share
their lives together. Grant them joy on their wedding day and
your happiness in their future together; through Jesus Christ,
whose presence brought such joy at Cana.

(John 2: 1–11)   *Kenneth Thornton*

376   THOSE JUST MARRIED, AND THEIR PARENTS

O God, whose Son Jesus Christ shared at Nazareth the life of
an earthly home, we pray that he may be acknowledged as head
of the household of these your children. And, as he found his
authority in serving, so may they learn to serve one another
in love.

We remember too the homes from which they have come,
and pray that you will bless those who have given N. and N. to
each other; through Jesus Christ our Lord.

(Luke 2: 39–40, 51)   *Worship Now*

377   LIFE TOGETHER

O gracious and merciful Father, by whose appointment
marriage has been given to the human race and by whose blessing
it is strengthened and sustained: we pray for N. and N., now
joined as husband and wife.

Keep them loyal and steadfast to each other. May their love know no doubt or change, but may shared tasks, trials, and joys bind them ever more closely in heart; through Jesus Christ our Lord.

Worship Now

GOD'S BLESSING ON A CIVIL MARRIAGE 378

Holy Father, the giver of all that is good, we thank you
    for the institution of marriage,
    for the honour of its estate,
    for the sacredness of its obligations, and
    for your Creator's gift of love between man and woman.
Send your Holy Spirit, we pray, upon . . . and . . .,
    who have been joined in this holy bond.
Strengthen them by your grace as they ask for your blessing
    upon their union as husband and wife.
Deepen their commitment to each other,
    and to Jesus Christ, in whose name we pray.

Orders & Prayers for Church Worship

THE NEWLY MARRIED 379

O God, in your word you have compared marriage to the perfect union between Jesus your Son and the church, his bride.

Be present we pray with all those newly married, as they set up a new home together.

Grant them lasting faithfulness to you and to each other; true unity with you and with each other; increasing love for you and for each other.

May they remember that unless the Lord builds the house the builders' work is all in vain.

And may their homes be places where others may meet with yourself; through Jesus Christ our Lord.

(Rev. 21: 2; Ps. 127: 1)   *C. Idle*

380 NEWLY MARRIED

God of love, from whom comes every good and perfect gift:
Bless *N.* and *N.* whom you have joined together in marriage;
May their home be radiant with joy and peace; and may all
    that is good and pure grow within its walls;
Give them wisdom for the daily affairs of life;
Bless them in time to come in the ordering of their family;
And keep them in their going out and in their coming in;
        through Jesus Christ our Lord.

Frank Colquhoun

MARITAL DIFFICULTIES

381 WHEN THINGS ARE GOING WRONG

Holy Spirit, be present, we pray, in homes
    where there is tension or anger,
    where partners find the other to have
        faults they had not expected, or
        habits they find it hard to tolerate.
Help each to look upwards at Jesus,
    to see him in the perfection that is his alone,
    to see his suffering for others' sins,
    to see his forgiveness for the repentant,
    to see all the possibility of new life in him.
Help each to look inwards at self,
    confessing sin and claiming the Saviour's mercy.
Then help each to look at the other partner
    in fresh humility and in renewed love,
    and to be restored in harmony and unity
        as heirs together of the gift of life,
           in Christ the Lord.

(Heb. 12: 2; 1 Pet. 3: 7)   *J. C.*

382 MARRIAGE GUIDANCE COUNSELLORS

O God our Father, whose Son our Lord blessed the
marriage at Cana in Galilee by his presence and the first of his
miracles; hear our prayer for all who seek to counsel those whose
marriages are at risk.

Give them sympathy, understanding, and insight into the needs of others; and so use them in this ministry that by your grace hurts may be healed, faults forgiven, and misunderstandings removed.

All this we ask in the name of Jesus Christ our Saviour.

(John 2: 1–11)   *Llewellyn Cumings*

THE DIVORCED   **383**

O Lord, we pray for all those
    who, full of confidence and love,
    once chose a partner for life, but
    who are now alone, after final separation.
May they have the grace of the Holy Spirit's ministry, so that
    hurt and bitterness are overcome by healing and love,
    personal weakness by your strength, and
    inner despair by the joy of knowing you
        and serving others,
            through Jesus Christ our Lord.

Susan Williams

MEDICAL WORKERS

THE MINISTRY OF HEALING   **384**

Loving Lord Jesus, in your earthly ministry
    you healed sick bodies
        and brought health to troubled minds.
Bless, we pray, all who are continuing your work
    in clinics and hospitals, here and throughout the world.
Give inspiration to those researching
    new ways to combat disease.
Give patience and sympathy to doctors and health visitors
    as they listen to patients and advise them.
Give skill to the hands and minds
    of surgeons as they operate.
Give endurance and compassion to nurses and to all
    who care for the sick and who follow in your steps,
            our Healer and Redeemer.

✝ CHURCH'S M. OF M.   *Beryl Bye*

385   LOVING AND CARING

O God, the source of life and health,
    we pray for all who are ill.
Give to their doctors and nurses
    love and care for them, and
    skill to make them well again.
In their illness may they learn more
    of your own love and care for them;
                        in Jesus Christ our Lord.

M. H. Botting's collection

386   SERVING THE SICK

Holy Spirit, promised Counsellor, we pray for those who are
called to the ministry of nurse, doctor, or hospital administrator,
and also for those who, without special training, bear heavy
burdens at home in looking after the ill and elderly. We
remember those who have to manage somehow on their own, and
ask your blessing on all the ordinary folk who are good
neighbours and friends in need.

In the bearing, and the alleviating, of human pain may the
Father's will be done, may the Father's love be known, and may
his grace be mighty to help; through Jesus Christ, his Son, our
Lord.

Jamie Wallace

MENTAL ILLNESS

387   CHRIST THE HEALER

O Lord Jesus Christ, by whom one who wandered among
the tombs was healed and clothed and converted:

We pray for your gift of mental health for those who suffer
in mind, for any reason and to any degree. Grant them release
from the tyranny of themselves, to enjoy the freedom and power
of a character made complete by knowing you.

To those who care for them and try to cure them, give
wisdom, skill, and unfailing love; for your own name's sake.

(Mark 5: 1–20)   *C. Idle*

DEPRESSION 388

O Lord, who shouldered the strain and the stress of life, be with those who because of their burdens go down into the pit of disturbance and depression. When things are black and hopeless stretch out your hand to hold them firm. Give them courage to climb upwards to the light of this world's day, and of your love; through Jesus Christ our Lord.

Marjorie Hampson

THE SUFFERERS 389

O God, the maker of men's minds and healer of their ills: bless all your children who suffer from mental illness; help them to trust you even on the darkest days; help them to know you in their deepest need; in your mercy release them from the causes of their sickness, that they may love and serve you with all their strength, with all their heart, and with all their mind; through Jesus Christ our Lord.

Dick Williams

THOSE WHO FIGHT MENTAL DISEASE 390

Lord of all power and might, bless those who try to heal the disordered minds of men.

Teach them first to study the mind of Christ, and inspire them to love this study best of all.

In their exploration of the minds of men help them to be so secure in their own grasp of reality that their spiritual perception, their strength of will, and their soundness of purpose may sustain them in their toil and give them good success; for the sake of those who suffer and of the Lord Jesus who cares for them.

Dick Williams

STEWARDSHIP

391   A TRUST FROM GOD

Guard us, O Lord,
>   from the wrong use of money;
>   from selfishness, carelessness, or waste; and
>   from that obsessive love of money
>   which is a root of all evil.
Enable us
>   to be good stewards of what is entrusted to us;
>   to give, or spend, or save, according to your will,
> so that neither poverty nor wealth
>   may hinder our discipleship,
>   harm our neighbours, or
>   destroy our life;
>   through Jesus Christ our Lord.

(1 Cor. 4: 1–2)   *C. Idle*

392   THE RIGHT USE OF WEALTH

Help us and all people, dear Lord,
>   to understand the purpose and place of money
>   in our life;
>   keep before us the peril of loving it;
>   help us to make it our servant,
>   and never our master.
And let neither the lack of it,
>   nor the possession of it,
>   in any degree loosen our grasp upon reality,
>   which is ours through love of Jesus Christ our Lord.

(1 Tim. 6: 10)   *Dick Williams*

THE PRAYER LIFE

LEARNING HOW TO PRAY 393

O Lord, you have commanded us to pray, and
      have promised to hear our prayers and
      answer them according to your will.
Teach us how to pray, and help us always to make the most
  of the opportunities we are given.
May we use these times
      to confess our sins to you,
      to ask your forgiveness,
      to thank you for all your goodness, and
      to make requests for others and not just for
        ourselves;
          through Jesus Christ our Lord.

(John 16: 23–4; 1 John 3: 22 & 5: 14–15)   *John Eddison*

DIFFICULTIES IN PRAYER 394

Lord, teach us how to pray with our hearts as well as with our lips. Keep our thoughts from wandering, and help us to remember that you are near us when we pray, and always ready to hear.

If our prayers are not always answered in the way we would like, give us grace to accept your will for us, and to remember that you know best.

Even when our life is busy, and our time is crowded with everyday activities, help us still to make time to turn to you for the strength and guidance we need, through Jesus Christ our Lord.

John Eddison

TRAVEL

395   TRAVELLING WITH CHRIST'S PRESENCE

Lord Jesus Christ, you travelled once
               by hard and dangerous roads;
               you drew near to your friends as they
               journeyed on the way,
                    both going along with them, and
                    sharing with them your truth:
Be present, we ask, with those who travel this week
     (especially . . .);
          guard them in every danger;
     make them aware that you are with them; and
     bring them safe and well to where they want to be;
               for your own name's sake.

(Luke 24: 15)   *C. Idle*

WITHOUT CHRIST

396   STRANGERS TO CHRIST'S LOVE

God and Father of us all, you loved the world so much
          that you gave your only Son
               for the salvation of mankind:
We pray for those who are strangers to your love;
          for those in spiritual darkness
               who have not heard the gospel of Christ; and
          for those who, having heard it,
               have chosen darkness rather than light.
In your great mercy draw them to yourself
          through him who was lifted up on the cross,
     that they may receive the gift of eternal life in him,
          our Lord and Saviour Jesus Christ.

(John 3: 14–18)   *Llewellyn Cumings*

CONVERSION TO CHRIST 397

God of grace and mercy,
open the eyes of the blind;
breathe life into the dead;
release those bound by sin and Satan.
Through your Holy Spirit's power
may hearts be challenged,
minds convinced, and
wills conquered;
In the name of Jesus, the Lord.

Michael Saward

YOUTH

GOD'S WORD TO THE CHURCH 398

Lord, let us never forget your promise
'Your sons and daughters will prophesy . . .,
your young men will see visions'.
Help us to remember that this is part of your purpose
to pour out your Spirit on all people.
Deliver us from the peril of quenching the Spirit
by failing to heed what he says to the whole church
through its young people;
in Christ's name.

(Joel 2: 28; Acts 2: 17; 1 Thess. 5: 19) *J. C.*

399   ACROSS THE GENERATION GAP

In order to understand the problems of young people, Lord,
    help us to consider
    the insecurity of the world in which they live today;
    the talk of war, and the practice of it;
    the affluence of so much of society, and the
        encouragement it gives them
            to possess and not to give;
    the unbelief in spiritual things
        among so many who shape their education;
    the strain of examinations;
    the uncertainty about whether
        there will be work for them even if they pass;
    the propaganda of so many kinds
        to which they are subjected.
All these things are stumbling blocks which their elders have
    set up against them.
So we thank you, Lord, for the vision and courage of so
                    many young people today;
            for their hatred of hypocrisy, and
                for their search for the truth.
May those who are young be helped
    to blend what is practicable
        with what they believe to be ideal;
    may those who were once young
        be ready to learn as well to teach; and
    may we all continually grow
        in the knowledge of your truth and
            in our obedience and loyalty
                to our Lord and Saviour, Jesus Christ.

Dick Williams

400   THE BIG DECISIONS IN LIFE

O God our Father, bless we pray
    the young people of our church;
        keep them faithful to you
            when the world beckons in the opposite direction;
        guide them in the great decisions they have to take
                concerning a career and choice of marriage partner;
        uphold them when they find it hard to get employment;
        and grant that in you they may find true peace.

Armed with your Spirit
   may they then do great things for you,
      for the sake of Jesus Christ our Lord.

Andrew Warner

A PARISH YOUTH GROUP   401

Lord of the church, we pray that you will bless and keep
      the members of the youth group of our parish.
May they be committed to you as Saviour,
   and be held together in common loyalty to you as Lord.
May they be in harmony with each other,
   and be effective in witness, together or alone.
May they recognize themselves as an integral part
      of the body of Christ here,
   and be ready to share
         in the responsibilities and privileges
         of the whole church.
And may all of us be helped
   to welcome the unfamiliar,
   to guide the inexperienced, and
   to give ourselves in service
   to our fellow-members of your church,
      to the glory of your name.

J. C.

YOUTH LEADERS   402

Heavenly Father, we thank you for calling members of our parish to be leaders among the youth, and we pray for your continued blessing on them in this ministry.

Help them to give encouragement and to show integrity, both by their teaching and by their example.

So strengthen them, deepen their vocation, and increase their understanding, that fruit may be brought forth to your glory.

(Titus 2: 6–8)   *J. C.*

SOCIETY AND STATE

CHRIST BE NEAR . . . **403**

Christ be near at either hand,
Christ behind, before us stand,
Christ with us where'er we go,
Christ around, above, below.

Christ be in our heart and mind,
Christ within our soul enshrined,
Christ control our wayward heart,
Christ abide and ne'er depart.

Christ our life and only Way,
Christ our lantern, night and day,
Christ be our unchanging friend,
Guide and Shepherd to the end.

David Adam after Saint Patrick

THE CHURCH OF IRELAND **404**

Grant, heavenly Father, that we and all the members
    of this Church of Ireland,
        whether individually,
            or in its synods, councils, and parishes,
    may always so speak and act that we shall be
        like the salt of the earth and
        like the light of the world.
May it be our aim
    to profess the faith of Christ
        as professed by the early church and
    to set forward quietness, peace, and love
        among all Christian people.
May these things for which we aim
        be those to which we attain,
    by your grace working in us what is pleasing to you,
        through Jesus Christ,
            to whom be glory for ever and ever.

(Matt. 5: 13–14; Heb. 13: 21)   *J. C.*

The second petition alludes to the 'Preamble and Declaration' adopted in
1870 at the disestablishment of the Church of Ireland.

405 A PRAYER FOR HARMONY

Gracious God, you have promised to make all things new:
We ask that you will fulfil this promise in Ireland,
  praying that you will
    give repentance to those who are prisoners of sin,
    restore love where there has been hatred,
    renew trust where there has been suspicion,
    send peace where there has been conflict,
    relieve suffering where there has been violence,
    grant serenity where there has been fear, and
    recreate concord in our midst;
      for the good of our children, and
      for the future of our community.
In the name of Jesus,
  in whom all that counts is a new creation.

(Rev. 21: 5; Gal. 6: 15)   *Michael Saward*

FOR USE IN THE REPUBLIC OF IRELAND

406 PRESIDENT AND COUNTRY

  Almighty God, the ruler of all nations, we ask you to look
with mercy upon our President and his ministers; that they may
ever use the authority which you have given to them for the peace
of the world, for the safety, honour, and welfare of the nation,
and for the good of your holy church; through Jesus Christ our
Lord.

Diocese of Central Tanganyika

407 THE PRESIDENT AND THOSE IN AUTHORITY

Lord God almighty, bless our President
  and all in authority under him;
    may godliness be their guidance;
    may sanctity be their strength;
    may peace be the fruit of their labours,
      and joy in heaven their eternal gift;
        through Jesus Christ our Lord.

Dick Williams

GOVERNMENT AND DEPUTIES 408

O God, your rule extends over all the earth, yet you have committed authority to the leaders of the nations.

Grant to the Taoiseach and to all members of the cabinet the insight, compassion, and courage that will enable them effectively to meet the demands of these days.

To all members of the Oireachtas give wisdom and humility as they take counsel together, that their decisions may promote the well-being of the nation and more nearly express your will; through Jesus Christ our Lord.

John Poulton

GARDA AND DEFENCE FORCES 409

Lord God, we remember before you the men and women serving in all ranks in the Garda Siochana and in our defence forces. Give them courage and resolution in times of crisis and danger, and skill, perseverance, and good humour in all that they have to do.

May those who exercise command remember always that they are your servants; may those whom they direct always act as men and women under authority.

Help us all by thought and deed constantly to encourage them in the faithful discharge of their calling;
through Jesus Christ our Lord.

D. R. Woodman

FOR USE IN NORTHERN IRELAND

410   THE QUEEN

Grant, O Lord, to her Majesty the Queen
    simple faith to walk in the way set before her,
    patience and courage to bear the burden laid upon her,
    humility to know that her sovereignty is but lent by you,
    and the sure hope of eternal life with you,
to whom belongs all dignity and greatness,
                all majesty and power,
                      both in this world and in that which
                      is to come.

Simon H. Baynes

411   THE ROYAL FAMILY

Almighty God, the source of all goodness:
As her subjects, and yours, we ask you to bless
    our gracious Queen Elizabeth,
    the Duke of Edinburgh,
    the Prince and Princess of Wales,
    Prince William,
    and all the Royal Family.
Empower them with your Holy Spirit;
enrich them with your heavenly grace;
prosper them with all happiness; and
bring them to your everlasting Kingdom;
through Jesus Christ our Lord.

Adapted from Book of Common Prayer

PRIME MINISTER AND PARLIAMENT

Bless our Prime Minister, O Lord, those who bear office **412** under the crown, and all members of Parliament, and strengthen them in their great responsibilities.

Put far away from them any cheap desire for personal gain or party advantage; unite them in seeking the safety, honour, and welfare of our Queen and country.

May they not conduct their debates or reach their decisions relying upon their own frail human wisdom, but upon that which comes to all who seek to follow you and to walk in your ways, through Jesus Christ our Lord.

John Eddison

THE COMMONWEALTH   **413**

We thank you, O Lord, for the Commonwealth, and that so many millions of men and women are united in their loyalty to the Queen and in their love of freedom and justice.

Help us to play our part, however small it may be, in making it an increasing force for good in the world. Teach all who belong to it to seek first your kingdom and righteousness, that it may become an instrument for your purpose in the world, and its influence used for the benefit of all mankind, through Jesus Christ our Lord.

John Eddison

We pray, O Lord, for those who are responsible for the maintenance of law and order in our community; for those who administer justice in the courts; and for those who are the victims of crime, violence, and deceit.

R. Lord, hear us.

We pray for all prisoners, especially for those who are facing long sentences, and for those who have lost faith in themselves and their fellow-men, and have little hope for the future.

R. Lord, hear us.

We pray for all those who have the custody and care of prisoners, for prison governors, officers, chaplains, visitors, and social workers.

R. Lord, hear us.

We pray for our Secretary of State, for ministers and civil servants, and for the commanders and members of our security forces.

R. Lord, hear us.

We pray for all those who have a special concern for the families of prisoners and for the after-care of offenders, and for all who try to find or provide employment for them.

R. Lord, hear us.

We pray for those who have been released from prison; for those who have managed to make good, and for those who remain unrepentant or who find the going hard.

R. Lord, hear us.

We pray for young people; for those who have already come up against the law; for those on probation, and for those on the fringe of illegal activities.

R. Lord, hear us.

We pray for parents, teachers, youth leaders, clergy, and all who try to help young people to escape from the sordid and the second rate and to find a true purpose in life; we ask that we may learn to be as forgiving of others as we trust that you are of us.

R. Lord, hear us.

We pray for ourselves as members of the community; and we ask that we may be kept with a right respect for law and order, and that this may not lessen our compassion and concern for those who have failed to live up to the standards you require in our society.

R. Lord, hear us.

Liverpool Cathedral

THE PROBLEMS OF NORTHERN IRELAND

415   PEACE AND RECONCILIATION

O Father, who makes men to be of one mind
in their homeland,
bring peace to the tragedies of Northern Ireland;
where neighbour may rise up against neighbour,
where familiar streets may become battlefields,
where familiar fields may become
places of ambush, and
where familiar people may become the casualties.
Change the hearts of all those who think that
their cause is more important
than another man's right to live;
Change such policies of those on either side which
may create, condone, or extend conflict.
By the power of the cross help
all who sin to repent, and
all who have been sinned against to forgive,
that peace and reconciliation may come;
through Jesus Christ our Lord.

Dick Williams

416   INDIVIDUAL RESPONSIBILITY

Living God, your Son Jesus Christ lived and worked
in this world;
he knew its hatred and war, its diseases and its sin.
Help us all to find a way out of deadlock to progress,
a way out of division to harmony,
a way out of selfishness to co-operation,
a way out of death to life.
Grant to us wisdom, restraint, and
a desire for fair and just dealing.
Channel the strong desire for peace among many people
into useful and constructive ways of peace-making;
and bring your own rule of peace
among those created in your image;
through Jesus Christ our Lord.

C. Idle

(When this prayer is used outside Northern Ireland, the words 'us all' in
the first petition may be altered to 'the people of Northern Ireland'.)

'ONE NEW MAN' 417

Father, we pray for our Province,
>   our politicians and our people;
> for the imagination and the will
> so to seek reconciliation and justice
>   as to find stable government and peace.
Grant that, as the Holy Spirit worked at first,
>   breaking down the dividing wall
>   between Jew and Gentile,
>   creating one new humanity in Christ,
> so by the same Spirit Protestants and Roman Catholics
>   may find in Christ the freedom
>   to share with one another, and
>   to care for each other in his name.

(Eph. 2: 14–15)   *Anon.*

(When used outside Northern Ireland, this prayer may be amended by the
substitution for the wording above the opening words 'Father, we pray for
Northern Ireland, its politicians and its people'.)

THE VICTIMS OF VIOLENCE 418

Our loving and caring Father, so often we see how
>   the violence of a few creates victims among the many:
We lift up before you all these victims, remembering
> all those who have been bereaved or physically hurt;
> all those who have been robbed
>   of livelihood or belongings;
> all those who suffer reactions of bitterness or fear.
We thank you that the perfect love of our Lord Jesus Christ
>   met death by violence and was not extinguished.
May he so enter the hearts and minds of all victims that
> frailty may be made good by his strength,
> loss by his riches, and
> bitterness by his total and victorious love,
>   for your name's sake.

Susan Williams

CITIZENSHIP IN A CHANGING SOCIETY

419   THE SALT OF THE EARTH

Lord Jesus, you challenged your disciples by telling them
                    that a city set on a hill cannot be hidden.
We pray for ourselves and for all
            who have been baptised in the name
                of Father, Son, and Holy Spirit,
        that in our generation and in today's world
            we may not be afraid
                to declare before men
                    the God whose we are and whom we serve;
            we may not be ashamed
                to bear witness to your gospel of salvation
                    for everyone who believes;
            we may not grieve the Holy Spirit
                by living before men in ways that deny his grace
                    in sealing us for the day of redemption.
Give us all so much greater a perception
    of what you have done for us, and
        so much greater a love
            for all who still do not know you,
    that we are resolved by your daily grace
            not to serve the gods that men raise up, and
            not to lose the saltiness of the salt of the earth;
                that your name may be glorified in our land.

(Matt. 5: 13–14 & 28: 19; Dan. 3: 18; Acts 27: 21–3;
Rom. 1: 16; Eph. 4: 30)   *J.C.*

420   PLAYING OUR PART IN SOCIETY

Almighty and everlasting God:
        Grant to each of us a right interest in the administration
            of our community and country;
        where we have a vote,
            help us to use it wisely;
        where we could serve on a board or committee,
            help us not to shirk responsibility;
        where we have a duty to attend a meeting,
            save us from lethargy.

We confess that we often grumble and complain of injustices,
    but don't do anything to try to put them right.
We confess that we often criticize others
        for actions they take,
    but take no action ourselves.
Stir us up, Lord,
    that our concern may lead us to prayer,
    and our prayer to loving service;
                in the name of Christ.

Beryl Bye

RIGHT THINKING AS THE SPRING OF RIGHT ACTIONS **421**

We pray, Lord, that all men may learn to seek first the
    Kingdom of God and his righteousness, caring for justice
    more than gain, and for fellowship more than for
    domination.
    R. Lord, hear us.
We pray that all may have the courage and the energy to
    think for themselves strongly and clearly, and to seek for
    the truth and follow it whatever the cost.
    R. Lord, hear us.
We pray for deliverance from prejudice and for a desire to
    appreciate what is just and true in the opinions of those
    who differ from us.
    R. Lord, hear us.
We pray that all may have the faith to believe that whatever
    is right is always possible, and that whatever is according
    to the mind of Christ can call upon the limitless resources
    of your power.
    R. Lord, hear us.
We pray that in ourselves and in others suspicion may give
    place to trust, and bitterness to goodwill; and that we all
    may become worthy of trust.
    R. Lord, hear us.
And finally we pray that God will grant peace in our time,
    and give us abundantly of his Holy Spirit, whose fruits
    are love, joy, and peace. Amen.

(Matt. 6: 33)   *William Temple*

422   SERVING THE UNWANTED

Lord God, source of cleansing and author of real life:
  remember those who work in your name
        among the outcast and unwanted men and women
        of our world.
Give them the faith to believe that you alone
        can cleanse filthy souls, stained by sin and degradation,
    and can remake shattered lives, broken by disobedience,
        to your glory and their joy,
            through our Saviour Jesus Christ.

Michael Saward

423   THOSE WHO SERVE THE COMMUNITY

We thank you, our Father, for those whose work sustains
our society and this community in which we live; for all who
create the wealth by which we trade, for those who grow and
provide our food or who, in industry, commerce and transport,
bring it to our homes.

We thank you for those who, day and night, maintain the
public services; for the police, for those who respond to
emergencies, and for all whose work is in health or healing or
social care.

Teach us to remember that all our lives depend upon the
work of many minds and hands; and we pray that we may live
thankfully and in unity as members of one human family;
through Jesus Christ our Lord.

Timothy Dudley-Smith

DIVISIONS IN SOCIETY 424

Give to us all, O God,
  wherever we stand in our present disagreements,
  a clear vision of the things we believe to be right and
  a great patience with the people we believe to be wrong.
Use your church in these days,
  and make her fit to be used.
May her counsel be far-seeing,
  her judgments temperate, and
  her way with people gentle;
    as befits the gospel she proclaims, in Christ's name.

Jamie Wallace

RACIAL HARMONY 425

Lord Christ, you are our peace, for by your cross you have broken down the dividing wall of hostility between the races.

By the power of your Spirit reconcile us to the Father and to our brothers and sisters of every colour and culture; that we may no longer be strangers to one another, but fellow-citizens with God's people and members of God's household, for the glory of your name.

(Eph. 2: 14–19)   *Frank Colquhoun*

DISCRIMINATION 426

Almighty God, creator and upholder of all things,
  take from our hearts that hatred
    which judges others by the colour of their skin, or
    which condemns them for their class or their
      denomination.
In its place, may love and justice prevail
  for the good of all humanity, and
  for the sake of Jesus Christ, who gave himself for all.

Michael Saward

SPIRITUAL RENEWAL IN SOCIETY

427   THE NATION'S GREATEST NEED

Lord of the nations, awaken us to all your word tells us
    about what you require in society!
Deliver us from being complacent in Zion
    when the moral fabric of the nation rots away!
Show us afresh that you have standards
    of right and wrong among men
        that we spurn at our peril!
Open our eyes to the true meaning
    of the signs of your displeasure
        at what is wrong in our nation!
Teach us again that you despise
    religion without righteousness!
Help us to seek good, not evil;
    to maintain justice, not self-interest.
In your mercy grant to the nation
    early repentance
    and restoration to your favour;
        through Jesus Christ, your Son, our Saviour.

(Amos 6: 1; 2: 6–8; 4: 6–11; 5: 21–4; 5: 14–15; 9: 11–15)   *J. C.*

428   REPENTANCE AND TRANSFORMATION

Father in heaven, whose will it is that all should
    worship you in the fellowship of your church, and
    serve you in the life of your world:
Send down upon our people a true spirit of repentance,
    for the rejection of your commandments
        which is called broadmindedness;
        for the apathy which is disguised as tolerance;
    for the intolerance
        whose true nature is contempt for others; and
    for the greed which glories in material things
        and grasps for more of them.
With sorrow for these sins, Lord God,
    send faith and obedience, so that
        lives may be transformed and renewed, and
    our society may be characterized
        by integrity and godliness:
        to your praise and glory,
        through Jesus Christ our Lord.

Michael Saward

THE DAILY WORKPLACE

FOR THE LORD'S SAKE 429

Thank you Lord for the gift of work,
    and for strength to do it.
Thank you for our brains and senses,
    and for the strength in our limbs and bodies.
Help us to use all these for you,
    to work well with our people,
    to make the place where we work a happier place,
    and
    to make the work of others
      easier and more pleasant for them.
Be with all who find work difficult or dull,
    who are surrounded by arguments and disputes,
      and
    who are exposed to especial dangers.
Bless those for whom we work, and
    those who work for us;
      in the name of Jesus, carpenter and Saviour.

C. Idle

THOSE WHOSE WORK WE WOULD NOT LIKE TO DO 430

Lord Jesus, you were prepared to wash your disciples' feet.
Be with those whose work in society
    is unpleasant, difficult, and dangerous.
Bless those who work during hours
    when most of us would not want to.
Deliver us from being heedless of them
    or uncaring for them,
    and help us to be ready to serve,
      as you served and gave yourself for us.

(John 13: 4–5)   *J. C.*

431   A COMMON PURPOSE

We commit to you, O Lord, all those who are engaged in industry—in the board-room, in the offices, and on the shop-floor.

Remove all misunderstanding, injustice, and prejudice, and everything that can damage relationships between one man and another, between management and worker, employer and employee; and may sympathy, good will, and fair play prevail.

Help those whose work is dreary and monotonous to find contentment and a sense of purpose in what they do, and grant that we may always respect and honour those upon whose skill and industry depend the welfare and prosperity of our country, through Jesus Christ our Lord.

John Eddison

432   FOR INDUSTRIAL PEACE

Great God and Father of all, send the Spirit of your Son
             into the hearts and minds
                 of employers and their staffs,
      so that all shall remember
                 that they each have a Master who is in heaven and
                 that in him there is no favouritism,
                     either to victimize or to show partiality.
Lead all to yourself,
             to be your disciples,
                 and heirs of the kingdom of heaven.

(Eph. 6: 9)   *J. C.*

433   LABOUR RELATIONS IN INDUSTRY

Almighty and everlasting God,
      we pray for all engaged in industry.
Bless and give guidance to all meetings
      between employers and employees.
Remove all bitterness, distrust, and prejudice
      from their deliberations.

Give to all a spirit of tolerance,
        the desire to understand the other's point of view,
        and an earnest determination to seek for justice
        and for truth.
May all work together for the common good,
        through Jesus Christ our Lord.

                                        W. A. Hampson

TRADES UNIONS AND THEIR LEADERS   **434**

God our Father, we thank you for all that trades unions have achieved in the past to improve the wages and conditions of workers.

We ask you to bless and guide their leaders today, that they may use their powers wisely and well, and may contribute to justice in relations between employers and employees. May they have respect for others' points of view, and remember that no man is unimportant in your sight.

May all Christian members and leaders of trades unions look for your guidance in decisions they have to make, and have courage to walk in your ways and bring glory to your name; through Jesus Christ our Lord.

                                        Peter Markby

THE WORLD OF COMMERCE   **435**

Lord of all men, help those who are employers or proprietors
    of business
        to have a right view of their varied responsibilities—
        to remember that they are servants of their customers,
        to have right relations with their employees and their
            families,
        to deal fairly with their suppliers,
        to contribute to society as the law requires, and
        to play a right part in the community.
In all things, help them to remember
        that they have a Master in heaven,
            with whom is no favouritism, but infinite grace.

(Eph. 6: 9)   *J. C.*

UNEMPLOYMENT

436   REDUNDANCY

Bless, O Lord, all those who at the height of their powers
have been deprived of their jobs. Help them and their families to
adjust to this crisis, and in it to act together as a loving and
courageous team.

Grant that all who lose security of employment may find an
inner security in Christ and, always being engaged in his service,
may be led to full employment once again.

We pray for leaders in government, industry, and commerce, asking that they may be helped to plan humanely and act
responsibly in all that affects their fellow-men; through Jesus
Christ our Lord.

Dick Williams

437   EMBITTERMENT

We commend to you, Father of mercies,
    all who suffer through unemployment,
    all who would work if they could,
    all whose labour seems not to be needed.
Provide, we pray, for them and their families;
    grant that no bitterness of mind
        may blot out your love from their lives.
Show the rest of us in society more clearly
    how we can help others in need, and
    how we can help them find work again;
        for the sake of that workman who was
        your only Son, Jesus our living Saviour.

C. Idle

THE ARMED FORCES

JUSTICE AND PEACE   **438**

O God our Father, we pray for all who serve in the Forces. May they meet danger with courage, and all occasions with discipline and loyalty. Save them from the spirit of cruelty and revenge, that they may truly serve the cause of justice and peace; for the honour of your name.

David Silk

GOD'S CARE AND PROTECTION   **439**

To your care and protection, O Lord of hosts, we commend the men and women of our armed forces at home and overseas.

Defend them in the hour of danger; strengthen them in the fulfilment of their duty; and enable them to serve their country with loyalty, courage and honour; through Jesus Christ our Lord.

Frank Colquhoun

(In the Republic it may be appropriate to omit the words 'at home and overseas' at the end of the first clause.)

EDUCATION

440   SCHOOLS AND COLLEGES

Eternal God, you are the source of all truth,
                    the goal of knowledge, and
                    man's leader down paths of discovery
                          and learning.

May the wisdom of your Spirit be with all whose calling is
                    to teach, in this and every land;
          give them insight
                          into the needs and aspirations of students,
          humility to go on learning, even while they teach,
          wisdom to discern what is best in the old and the new,
                    and, above all,
          that grace and beauty of life
                    without which knowledge is vain;
                              for Christ's sake.

A Book of Prayers for Students (SCM)

441   TEACHERS AND LECTURERS

We commend to you, O Lord, all who teach
                    in our universities, colleges, and schools.
Give them a love and reverence for the truths you have
                    revealed,
                    skill in imparting their knowledge to others, and
                    sympathy and understanding for those they teach.
Above all, help them to remember
          that the fear of the Lord
               is the beginning of wisdom, and
          that all teaching and learning are incomplete
               that do not help us to see more clearly
                    your handiwork
                         in nature, art, and science,
                         and in the lives of men;
                              through Jesus Christ our Lord.

(Ps. III: 10; Prov. I: 7)   *John Eddison*

TEACHERS AND STUDENTS 442

Lord Jesus Christ, the source of all knowledge and truth, give to all who teach the spirit of wisdom and understanding, and grant that all who learn may have a true judgment in all things, that we might be an upright and God-fearing people, for your sake.

M. H. Botting's collection

STUDENTS 443

Grant, Lord, to all students
    to love that which is worth loving,
    to know that which is worth knowing,
    to praise that which pleases you most,
    to esteem that which is most precious to you, and
    to dislike that which is evil in your eyes.
Grant that with true discernment
    they may distinguish between things that differ,
    and, above all, may search out and do
        what is well-pleasing to you;
                    through Jesus Christ our Lord.

Thomas à Kempis

SCIENCE 444

We thank you, O Lord, for the wonders of science, and for all that man has been able to learn about himself, about this planet on which we live, and about the universe around us.

May these discoveries never make us proud, but deepen our reverence for you, the creator and preserver of all things, and strengthen our faith in your love and power.

Grant that we may never yield to the temptation to misuse our knowledge for selfish or unworthy purposes, but that it may always be devoted to the benefit of mankind and the glory of your name, through Jesus Christ our Lord.

John Eddison

445

EXAMINATIONS

We remember before you, O God of truth, all who are now facing examinations—especially those known to us, and those who know you.

Grant that they may readily remember all that they have honestly learned, and may give a true account of their ability.

Whatever may depend upon the results, help them to give their future willingly and trustfully to you;
through Jesus Christ our Lord.

C. Idle

ELECTIONS

446

THE ELECTORS

Lord God of the nations,
before whom there is no authority
except that which you establish,
and who has created us with the freedom and responsibility
of choosing whom we will serve:
Guide each voter in the coming election,
and over-rule in its outcome,
that in the mystery of the fulfillment of your will
there may be elected to office those who seek
others' good before their own,
the execution of policies that
conform to your will, and
the glory of your great name.

(Rom. 13: 1; Josh. 24: 15; Phil. 2: 4) *J. C.*

447

THE CANDIDATES

Lord, guide us all as we vote,
that those elected may be men and women
led by your Holy Spirit,
wise to discern between right and wrong,
patient to listen,
skilled and honest in speech,
courageous to stand alone when necessary,
healthy in mind and body.

Help them always to maintain a right relationship between
    the interests of the state,
    the problems or concerns of the individual,
    and loyalty to party policy or discipline;
for the good of church and society
and to the glory of your name.

J. C.

FARM LIFE

THOSE WHO WORK ON THE LAND 448

We pray, O Lord, for all who work on the land,
    for those who till the soil
    and tend the cattle,
    for gardeners, fruit-growers, and farmers.
We thank you for their devoted work
    at all times and in all weathers.
We ask you to protect them from misfortune and damage
    and to prosper their efforts so that in due time
    we may enjoy the fruit of their labours.
Grant them pride and pleasure in their work,
    that they may know that in cultivating the earth
    they are fulfilling your command and
    helping to meet the needs of mankind.
Finally, O Lord, give us thankful hearts,
    and make us grateful for all that we receive from you
    as a result of their labour and skill,
    through Jesus Christ our Lord.

John Eddison

449 PRODUCTION AND DISTRIBUTION OF FOOD

O Lord, our Lord,
> how majestic is your name in all the earth!
> You are creator of all,
> > yet you have set man
> > > as ruler over the works of your hands.
We pray for those whose work is on the land
> > or in the production of food for the nations;
> > bless them by sending the sun and the rain
> > > that the earth may be fruitful;
> > teach them their responsibility
> > > not to abuse your creation;
> > show them how to share your bounty with others
> > > and pass on a rich heritage to their children.
For to you belong all majesty and glory.

(Ps. 8)

J. C.

INFORMATION TECHNOLOGY

450 MASTER OR SERVANT?

Creator God, who has wonderfully formed us all and
> > the complex world in which we live,
> we thank you for your gifts of thought
> > which have enabled mankind
> > > to devise the instruments of today's information
> > > technology, and
> > > to foresee yet more amazing developments in the
> > > future.
In learning to use these tools,
> may we not allow respect for their capabilities
> > to overshadow a right reverence for your creation;
> may we not forget our responsibilities
> > for workers whose skills may be superseded;
> may we not belittle the personalities
> > of individual men and women;
> may we not assume that men are made for these inventions
> > rather than they as servants of men; and
> may we not use them for purposes of evil and destruction.

All this we ask in the name of him who reminded us
 that even the hairs of our heads are numbered and
  known to your Fatherly care,
   our Lord Jesus Christ.

(Luke 12: 7)   *J. C.*

LOCAL GOVERNMENT

THOSE WHO SERVE THE COMMUNITY   **451**

Grant to us Lord that our community leaders,
 elected representatives, and local government staff
  may be men and women who
   remember that they are called to serve,
   understand the cares and joys of ordinary people,
   are concerned for the common good, and
   are skilled in knowing the law and applying it fairly;
    for Christ's sake.

(Mark 10: 43)   *J. C.*

ENHANCEMENT OF THE COMMUNITY   **452**

Heavenly Father, we pray for all who serve our community,
 in elected, salaried, or voluntary office.
Bless every effort they make
 to work together in harmony,
 to increase the prosperity of our district,
 to enhance the beauty of our environment, and
 to help those in need;
  for the sake of him
   whose heart went out to the needy,
    our Lord Jesus Christ.

(Luke 7: 13)   *J. C.*

THE MASS MEDIA

453   ALL COMMUNICATORS

Great God, you have made your Son known to us as
  the Word:
Inspire those whose work is
  the communication of words and ideas
              through television,
              through radio, and
              through the printed page.
May they use their gifts and opportunities
    to build rather than to destroy,
    to heal rather than to hurt,
    to purify rather than to corrupt;
That the good news of Jesus Christ may be heard
    throughout the world:
                    in whose name we pray.

(John 1: 1, 14)   *Michael Saward*

454   TELEVISION

Lord God, you have placed in human hands
            great power for good or evil through television:
We pray for
      those whose faces and voices are known
        in millions of homes;
      those who decide policies and plan schedules; and
      those who direct and produce programmes.
We pray
      that their skills and gifts may be devoted
        to what is true and good, and
      that those who watch and listen
        may be informed and entertained
            without being debased or corrupted;
                through Jesus Christ our Lord.

                                                    C. Idle

We thank you Lord for the gift of entertaining others which you have given to so many, on stage and screen, on radio and television, and in sport.

Help them never to misuse it by stooping to unworthy humour or unfair play, for the sake of cheap laughter or unworthy motives; instead may they use this gift for your glory and for the good of their fellow-men.

Grant too that we who watch may be refreshed and uplifted by what they do, and may return more keenly and readily to our work, through Jesus Christ our Lord.

John Eddison

THE PHILOSOPHIES OF MEN

MATERIALISM **456**

O God, in your love you have bestowed on us gifts such as our fathers never knew or dreamed of.

In your mercy grant that we may not be so occupied with material things that we forget the things which are spiritual; lest, having gained the whole world, we lose our own soul; for your mercy's sake.

(Mark 8: 36) *Daily Prayer*

457   TOTALITARIANISM

We plead with you today, O God,
    for those nations in East and West
        where totalitarian governments give little freedom.
For their leaders, we ask
    that they may learn to govern
        in justice, mercy, and truth;
For their people, we ask
    that they may be able to hear your gospel
        and heed your word;
And for all your servants in these lands, we pray for
        great faithfulness,
        great courage, and
        great love; through Jesus Christ our Lord.

C. Idle

458   THOSE FROM WHOM WE DIFFER

Lord, your love knows no bounds, no limits, no distinctions.

We pray for those from whom we differ in religion, in race, or in politics, asking that both we and they may be open to your revelation.

Help us to understand their points of view and to respect their rights to it.

As you are creator of all, teach us that every man is our neighbour.

Keep reminding us that it is because of your love for the whole world that you gave your only Son, that anyone who believes in him shall not perish but have the everlasting life for which we praise your name.

(John 3: 16)   *Adapted from Frank Colquhoun*

PRISONERS

FREEDOM THROUGH CHRIST 459

Almighty God, we remember the joy that you brought
  to the prison at Philippi,
    when your apostles prayed and sang your praises
      at midnight,
    when you delivered them from wrongful arrest, and
    when the jailer and his family believed
      and were baptized.
We praise you that the good news of Jesus Christ
      has still power to set men free from sin,
  and we ask that your Spirit
    may work in our prisons today,
      through the lives of those who know you,
      through the ministry of chaplains, and
      through the words of Scripture; ——— *+ prisoners of conscience etc*
        in the name of him whom you sent
        to proclaim freedom for the prisoners,
          our Lord Jesus Christ.

(Acts 16: 25–34; Luke 4: 18)   *J. C.*

PRISONERS AND DEPENDANTS 460

We pray, O Lord, for all those who have been imprisoned
        for crimes against society;
    care for them in their many different needs;
  to hardened criminals grant repentance;
  to the penitent give peace;
  to the confused give light;
  to all who suffer through separation from their families,
    give comfort.
Renew the hope and love of married people;
  turn the hearts of parents to their children
    and the hearts of children to their parents,
  and reunite them in your healing peace.
And be so present, O Lord, in the prisons of our land
  that many may call upon you
  and be made whole and free in Christ our Lord.

Dick Williams

461 THE MINISTRY OF STAFF

Lord God of love and mercy, we pray for our prisons;
　　for those detained in them, and
　　for those who work there.
May prison officers be kept safe,
　　and be helped truly to care for prisoners.
May governors and administrators be wise and just.
May chaplains and prison visitors
　　be richly endowed by the Holy Spirit.
May the guilty be brought to repentance from sin,
　　and to release into new life in Christ,
　　　　the only Saviour and Lord.

J. C.

ROAD SAFETY

---

462 LOVING OUR NEIGHBOUR

O God, who has taught us to love you, and to love our neighbours as ourselves, give to us and to all who use the roads—whether to drive, to ride, or to walk—consideration and care for others; that death and injury may be caused to no one, and that all who travel may go in safety, peace, and joy; through him who is the way, the truth, and the life, Jesus Christ our Lord.

(Luke 10: 27–8; John 14: 6)　　　　　　　　*Frank M. Best*

O Lord, we are often shocked and saddened when we hear of people of all ages being killed and injured on our roads; so we ask you to help all road-users not to relax proper care and attention.

Restrain those who want to drive when they are too tired, or are not in a fit condition to do so; hold back all who are tempted to enjoy speed for its own sake, or to behave selfishly, unkindly, and recklessly.

Help those who manufacture and maintain motor vehicles, that no carelessness on their part may add to the hazards and dangers.

So grant, O Lord, that through the efforts of all the number of accidents may be reduced, and with it the occasions of grief and suffering, through Jesus Christ our Lord.

John Eddison

SCIENCE

WISDOM, LEARNING, AND KNOWLEDGE   **464**

Great God, we praise you for the marvels of your creation,
    and for helping mankind to grow in knowledge of it.
We pray that you will keep us from forgetting
    the truth of the words
        'the fear of the Lord is the beginning of wisdom';
Deliver men and women from thinking
    that as they amass learning they grow in wisdom.
Enable us all to use our knowledge rightly—
    not for destruction and war, but
        as servants of our fellow-men and
        as stewards of your creation;
        to the glory of your name.

(Ps. 111: 10; Prov. 1: 7)   *J. C.*

465   INCREASED KNOWLEDGE; ITS USE AND MISUSE

We thank you, Lord, for this wonderful world
  with all its resources;
    so much recently discovered, so much yet to be found.
We thank you for the trained minds and patient personalities
        which harness nature's powers to human need;
    for swift travel and instant communication;
    for research into the causes and cure of disease;
    for space research into unknown worlds.
Accept our thanks, O Lord,
    and accept too our penitence
      for the many ways we use our knowledge
        for the destruction,
          suffering, and
          despair of mankind,
            rather than
      for the building up of life on earth
        in happiness and hope.
May your Holy Spirit pervade the minds
    of scientists and politicians in every land
  and shape the desires of men and nations,
      that your gifts may be a blessing, not a curse,
              through Jesus Christ our Lord.

Derek Williams

466   ADVANCED RESEARCH

God of all wisdom, Creator and Giver of life, we pray for all
who are engaged upon scientific research; may their work be
healthful and right in its aims, its methods and its uses.

Keep us all humble enough to know that we cannot answer a
question like that you put to Job, 'Where were you when I laid
the earth's foundation?'

In answer to it we can only offer you ourselves and our
worship, through Jesus Christ our Redeemer.

(Job 38: 4)   *J. C.*

SEAFARERS

THOSE AT SEA, AND AT HOME AGAIN   **467**

Lord almighty, we pray for those
  who go out on the sea in ships,
    who have seen your wonderful deeds in the deep,
    who may be in great peril,
    who also have known you to still the storm to a whisper.
Show them that there is no trouble
    in which they cannot cry out to you,
  and let them give thanks to you for your unfailing love.
Bring them safely home to harbour, and to their homes,
  and bless those who wait for them there;
                      for Christ's sake.

(Ps. 107: 23–31)   *J. C.*

THE LIFEBOAT SERVICE   **468**

Heavenly Father, we ask that your protection may rest upon those who man the lifeboats along our coasts. We pray for the wives, mothers, and sisters who see their menfolk go out, never knowing if they will return. Bless these men for their courage as they risk their lives for others with no thought of reward or gain, and remind us to support them through our prayers and gifts.

Beryl Bye

SOCIAL WORKERS

469   SEEING AS CHRIST SAW

God, our heavenly Father, you know our needs
   and you care for us all.
We pray for all who give support and counsel
      to their fellow-men;
         for youth workers and student advisors;
         for the Samaritans and other volunteers;
         for probation officers;
         for social workers; and
         for all others also who by their skill and training
            ease the burden of the aged, the lonely, and the
               perplexed, and
            guide those who have lost their way.
May they have both wisdom and sympathy,
   and see men through the eyes of Christ,
      who had compassion on the crowd
         because they were harassed and helpless,
            like sheep without a shepherd.
Grant all this for his sake, our Lord and Saviour.

(Matt. 9: 36)   *H. P. Leatherland*

470 '. . . THAT THOSE WHO LIVE SHOULD NO LONGER
LIVE FOR THEMSELVES'

We thank you Father for your gift of perfect love,
    Jesus Christ.
We thank you for all who have accepted your gift and in
        whom the light shines;
        for those who try to improve the plight of
           the homeless and badly housed;
        for young people sharing their learning and
           energy freely through voluntary service,
           at home and abroad;
        for all who help relieve suffering and
           distress;
        for those who live out your message in the
           midst of ignorance, fear and disease;
        for all who freely give their time, energy and
           money to bring comfort, hope, and help to
           those who need it.
We thank you Father that in the darkness the light still
        shines, and
        that Jesus is the true light.
Help us, we pray, to let our light shine before men,
    that they may praise you, our Father in heaven.

(John 1: 5 & 8: 12; Matt. 5: 16)   *Patricia Mitchell*

SPORTSMANSHIP

471   THE CHRISTIAN'S GOAL

We pray, Father, for all who engage in sports and contests,
      whether for their own pleasure
          or the entertainment of others, (especially . . .)
We pray that they may be kept from harm and injury.
We ask
      that through their knowledge of the laws of the game
          they may see that there are greater laws;
      that through their experience of training and restraint
          they may see that there is a nobler discipline;
      that through their desire for victory
          they may be directed to the greatest triumph of all
              and to the goal which is Christ,
                 the Saviour of the world.

(1 Cor. 9: 24–5)   *C. Idle*

WORLD NEEDS

THE KINGDOM OF GOD AMONG
THE NATIONS

UNDERSTANDING THE TIMES 472

Sovereign Lord of the nations,
    grant that we and all your people
        may be aroused
            to our responsibilities in your world,
        may by your grace be given
            understanding of the times,
        may know what we should do, and
        may be resolved to make Christ King,
            to his eternal glory.

(1 Chron. 12: 23, 32) *J. C.*

SHARING IN CREATION AND SALVATION 473

Creator God, you have made every nation of men
        that they should inhabit the whole earth,
    and have sent your dear Son to preach
        peace to those who were far away, and
        peace to those who were near:
Grant that the people of the world
        may reach out for you, and
        may find you,
    and hasten, O Lord, the fulfilment of your promise
        that you would pour out your Spirit on all people,
            for the sake of your name,
                on which all who call will be saved.

(Acts 2: 17–21 and 17: 26–7; Eph. 2: 17) *G. E. L. Cotton*

474   AWARENESS OF OTHERS' RIGHTS

We pray, O God, for our human brothers and sisters
    in parts of the world
        where the harshness of nature and the strife of the nations
    have brought sufferings longer and deeper
        than we have yet known.
We pray for the peoples of . . .
    and especially for those among them who are
            oppressed,
            in want, or
            forced to flee from home and family.
By the Spirit of Jesus, restrain and change
    those who seek their own advantage
        from others' sufferings.
Open the eyes of those of us who are so used to
            thinking of ourselves as always in the right and
            finding ourselves always comfortable
    that we do not see others' injustices and deprivations.
Make us followers, in deed as well as in word,
    of Jesus Christ, the Prince of Peace.

Jamie Wallace

475   THE SORROWING AND THE PERSECUTED

Dear Father, we ask you to uphold in faith
    all those who today are passing through dark shadows
        of sorrow, despair, or torment.
Give to them the spirit that
    sings your praise in a dungeon, and
    calls down blessings on those who persecute and slay.
Set free those who suffer,
    and give meanwhile the assurance deep in the heart
        that suffering is not waste, and
        that your purposes do not fail
            —nor your love
                in Jesus Christ our Lord.

Jamie Wallace

THE NATIONS AND THEIR LEADERS

WE HAVE ALL SINNED . . .   **476**

Almighty God, King and Judge of all mankind, look in pity upon the nations oppressed by strife, bitterness, and fear.

We acknowledge our share in the sins which have brought us so often to the brink of destruction.

May your goodness lead us to repentance, that we may yet again be spared.

Restrain the pride, the passions, and the follies of men, and grant us your grace, mercy, and peace;
through Jesus Christ our Saviour.

John R. W. Stott

RULERS' RESPONSIBILITIES   **477**

Lord God, we pray for those to whom you have entrusted
the power to rule among men.
Help them to remember their responsibility to you,
and to be so trustworthy in using it
until the day of account
that your kingdom shall be prospered
and they shall be found your good servants;
in Christ our Lord.

(Luke 19: 12–17)   *J. C.*

TRUE STATESMANSHIP   **478**

Almighty God, whose Son refuted the tempter's suggestion that he might receive the authority and the splendour of the kingdoms of the world by worshipping him as their master: grant that the statesmen of the nations may know that authority is not theirs to seize but yours to confer, and that the true splendour is for those who walk with our Saviour Jesus Christ and are clothed in heavenly glory, by his grace.

(Luke 4: 5–7; Rev. 2: 26; 3: 4, 5)   *J. C.*

479   LEADERS' DUTY TO SEEK PEACE

Grant Lord that among those who sit in high places
        there shall be many who shall be prepared
    to come as your children,
    to listen to your teaching,
    to learn the fear of the Lord,
    to turn from evil and do good, and
    to seek peace and pursue it,
        as humble followers of our Lord Jesus Christ.

(Ps. 34: 11–12)   *J.C.*

480   AT A TIME OF INTERNATIONAL CONFERENCE

O God, ruler of the destinies of men and nations, we thank
you for every happening which draws the peoples of the world
nearer together in fellowship and in purpose.

Grant to all representatives of nations who confer with one
another and on whose word and attitude so much depends, the
guidance of your Holy Spirit and the grace of humility that they
may be ready to see a point of view which differs from their own,
and keep before them not only the welfare of their own nation as
they see it, but your will for the whole world. Through Jesus
Christ our Lord.

Leslie D. Weatherhead

481   AT A TIME OF INTERNATIONAL CRISIS

God of all wisdom and might:
We pray for those involved in the present crisis in . . .,
    especially those who bear the responsibility and
                        exercise the authority of leadership.
May the Holy Spirit so direct their counsels and actions that
            justice and mercy may prevail,
            evil be averted, and
            harmony restored,
        to the honour of your great name;
            through Jesus Christ our Lord.

Frank Colquhoun

PEACE IN THE NEAR EAST

482

Lord and Creator of all the ends of the earth, we pray for peace among the children of Abraham.

Where Jew and Moslem and Christian are oppressed by their history and their hate, restrain the wicked and strengthen the peace-makers.

Where there are signs of hope and beginnings of understanding, grant perseverance.

Make us aware, beyond the defeats and despairs we bring upon ourselves, of your aching heart of love for all peoples, our one God and our Judge.

John Poulton

FOREIGN POLICIES OF THE NATIONS

THE COMMON GOOD

483

God and Father of all, you have taught us to care for one another and to live in peace; grant that our policies towards other nations may be dictated not by self-interest but by concern for the common good, and that we may seek to further the cause of justice and freedom in the world; through Jesus Christ our Lord.

(Rom. 12: 10–11, 18)   *James M. Todd*

NATIONALISM

484

Eternal God, ruler of all:
    Look upon those human societies
        which have set national pride and independence
           above all else;
    Help them to see that
        the peace of the world is more important
           than the glory of the nation;
    Enable them to seek
        your justice rather than their own prosperity;
That your name may be honoured, and
that their name may be respected
        among us all, for Christ's sake.

Michael Saward

THE UNITED NATIONS

485   THE RESPONSIBILITIES OF LEADERSHIP

Almighty God, we pray for the leaders of the United *S,*
~~Nations~~, and especially for those on whom rests great responsibility at the present time. *PRESIDENT BUSH + CABINET/ HOR*

Give them wisdom to make right decisions, courage to fulfil
them, and perseverance to continue their efforts to establish
peace and promote the welfare of humanity, to the glory of your
name.

Frank Colquhoun

PAUSE + REFLECT . . . .
NOT FROM ANGER, RETRABUTION AGAINST HOSTE
BINDING TOGETHER

486   ITS DIVERSITY OF ACTIVITIES

We pray Lord for the many agencies of
    the United Nations Organization.
We ask for your guidance in matters of political controversy,
    and your help for those involved in them.
We pray also for the many engaged upon the humanitarian
   projects about which we know so little;
     bless, we pray, all that is done for
       the relief of suffering,
       the improvement of agriculture,
       the spread of literacy, education, and culture,
       the safeguarding of human rights,
       the upholding of justice, and
       the promotion of better understanding between
         nations.
Through all such activities, may the Spirit of Christ
    be spread in your world;
       in his name we ask it.

J. C.

OVERSEAS MISSION

PRAYING FOR LABOURERS 487

Lord God, the harvest is plentiful, but the labourers are few.
So we pray that you, the Lord of the harvest,
    will send forth labourers into your harvest,
        to preach the good news to the nations,
        to build up your church in every land, and
        to serve the needs of mankind everywhere;
            for the sake of Jesus our Saviour.

(Matt. 9: 37–8)   *Frank Colquhoun*

THE IMPLICATIONS OF PARTNERSHIP 488

Lord God, as the church in Antioch heard from the apostles
    on their return home
        what you had done through them in other lands, and
        how you had opened the door of faith to others,
so may we receive with gladness news of your Holy Spirit
    at work today in the churches overseas,
and be ready to be called to more faithful prayer for them,
        to be impelled to most costly giving to them,
        and to be challenged to more effective
            discipleship ourselves
                because of your power at work in them.
                and by the grace of our Lord Jesus
                    Christ.

(Acts 14: 26–7)   *J. C.*

VOLUNTARY SERVICE OVERSEAS 489

God, whose Son Jesus Christ came to share our life on earth;
hear our prayer for all who give voluntary service overseas, that
in the spirit of Christ they may give of their best among those
with whom they work and live; and through their service may the
cause of peace in the world be strengthened; for the sake of our
Lord Jesus Christ.

                        David Silk

490   EXPATRIATES HELPING OVERSEAS CHURCHES

Eternal and ever-present God,
    be near to those who serve your church in other lands
        as enablers and sustainers of national leaders;
    help them to learn to take the hard and humble road
        of those who support rather than those who lead;
    uphold them as they work in cultures
        widely different from their own; and
    give them grace to live at peace
        in their hearts and their homes;
In the name of Jesus Christ.

Michael Saward

491   THE CHURCH IN A PARTICULAR COUNTRY

God and Father of our Lord Jesus Christ,
    we pray for your blessing on your church in . . .
May its members be your ambassadors,
    calling men to be reconciled with you
        through Christ,
        who loved us and gave himself for us.
As you showed your love
    by sending your Son into the world,
        so may its members love one another.
As they love one another,
    so may they live in obedience to you.
As they live in obedience to you,
    so may they discern and resist what is not from you.
As they resist what is evil,
    so may they do what is good.
As they do what is good,
    so may men see their deeds and praise you,
        our Father in heaven.

(2 Cor. 5: 20; 1 John 5: 9–11; 2 John 5–10; 3 John 11; Matt. 5: 16)   *J. C.*

ASIA **492**

O God, who called wise men from the east
  to bring their treasures to the feet of Christ:
Grant that the men of Asia
        may see a new star, and
        set out on a new pilgrimage;
So may they and all mankind meet at the feet of Christ;
            for his name's sake.

(Matt. 2: 1, 11)   *Dick Williams*

AFRICA **493**

    O God our Father, who gave to a man of Africa the privilege
of carrying the cross of Christ: give courage to the Christians of
Africa when they walk the road of ridicule and suffering; build
among them a church which is not ashamed of Jesus Christ,
nailed to the cross; for his name's sake.

(Luke 23: 26)   *J. Wheatley Price*

CHRISTIAN LITERATURE

A SOCIETY IN NEED **494**

As Jesus saw the crowds harassed and helpless,
        like sheep without a shepherd,
    so, our Father, call men and women today to see the needs
        for tending and nourishing those outside the church.
Give the vocation for publishing and distributing
        your word and all Christian literature;
    with it, give skills and the money
        to present the message of Jesus
            in a form that honours his name and
            attracts the reader to him.
So may the wandering be found and the needy fed,
            by the power of the Holy Spirit.

(Matt. 9: 36)   *J. C.*

495   WRITERS, PUBLISHERS, AND DISTRIBUTORS

Raise up in our day, O Lord, Christian writers
    who know you and your word, and
    who love and understand their fellow-men.
Teach them how to communicate through the printed word,
    and enable their work to be published and distributed.
So may men and women, boys and girls,
    know the good news of Jesus Christ, and
    be helped to live by him to your glory.

J. C.

FAMINE AND HUMAN NEED

496   MEASURES TO OVERCOME IT

O God our Father, in the name of him who gave bread to the
hungry we remember all who, through our human ignorance,
folly, selfishness, and sin, are condemned to live in want; and we
pray that all endeavours for the overcoming of world poverty and
hunger may be so prospered that there may be found food
sufficient for all. We ask this through Jesus Christ our Lord.

Christian Aid

497   THE NEEDS OF THE FASTING AND OF THE FEASTING

Dear Lord, look down upon the starving world, your world—
              the homeless men,
              the widowed women,
              the children desperate for food.
Have pity on those who fast—and have pity on us who feast;
Pity them, the pitiful—and pity us, the pitiless;
Have mercy on their starving bodies—and our starving souls;
              for Jesus' sake.

Simon H. Baynes

OUR OWN STEWARDSHIP 498

Almighty God, by your special providence you fed the people of Israel in the desert with the manna you sent for their daily needs, so that none had more and none had less than he required.

Send your Spirit into our selfish world today; by his grace teach us so to use and to share your gifts that our enjoyment of them may accord with our need for them.

So may the poor be filled, in Christ's name.

(Exod. 16: 18) *J. C.*

NOT FROM NATURAL CALAMITY ALONE 499

Great God, who requires righteousness in the nations,
  we remember before you some of the ways in which
    men turn the calamities of nature
      into famine and starvation—
the unwillingness of many landlords
    to forgo their rents;
the self-satisfaction of many bureaucrats,
    who see no need for special effort
      on behalf of others;
the corruption of many distributors of food,
    who see it as an opportunity for self-enrichment;
the preference of many specialists
    to use their skills only for themselves;
the greed of many taxpayers,
    who want above all to improve
      their own standard of living;
the self-interest of many politicians,
    who think of what will gain them votes.
While we do indeed pray that you will send rain
    upon the parched soils of so many lands,
  we pray too that you will pour out your Holy Spirit
    upon the dry hearts of sinful men.
For it is they, and we, who are responsible
  for so much of the suffering
    of men, created in your image, and
    of the children, who were loved and blessed
      by our Lord Jesus Christ.

J. C.

500   AT A TIME OF DISASTER

We commend to you, heavenly Father,
            the people of . . . in their need and distress.
Stir men's wills to send help to them speedily,
      and remove hindrances to this help
            reaching them in time.
Give strength, endurance, and health to all relief workers,
      and fill them with the love of Christ.
Grant that the needy may have what they require,
            both for their immediate needs,
            and for their longer-term rehabilitation;
                  in Christ's name.

J. C.

DEVELOPING COUNTRIES

501   MEDICAL WORKERS

Thank you, our Father, that your love has been the spur
      which has sent men and women with medical training
      to many places where sickness and disease are endemic.
            Strengthen them when they work long hours
                  with little rest.
            Guide them when they lack equipment
                  and medicines.
            Sustain them when they are tired.
            Encourage them when they are depressed.
            Protect them when they are in danger; and
            Augment their skills with your healing power.
That their loving service may bear witness
      to the Saviour who brings wholeness to a sick world.

Michael Saward

Lord of all wisdom,
 we pray for the many young people
  in the developing nations
  who crowd into their countries' schools, and
  who hope that by formal education
   they will secure for themselves
   prosperity and material benefits
   beyond their brothers.
Give them your help
 to realize that from him to whom much is given
  much shall be required, and
 to want to serve their fellow-men.
Spare them from the bitterness of disillusion
 when they find things not working out
  as they first expected.
Deliver them from the bondage of thinking
 that a man's life consists
  in the abundance of his possessions.
Grant that your word may be so ministered to them
 that they become rich toward God,
  by faith in the Saviour, Jesus Christ.

(Luke 12: 15, 21)   *J. C.*

ADULT LITERACY 503

Gracious God, who has caused the Scriptures to be written
  that men may believe that Jesus is the Christ;
We remember before you the millions in the world
  who are unable to read what is written.
We ask you to bless and further the labours
  of all who are committed to adult literacy work;
 that many more may become able to read,
 that your word may be readily available for them
  to read and understand in their own language, and
 that they may come to have new life
  in the name of your Son, the Saviour of the world.

(John 20: 21)   *J. C.*

RACIAL HARMONY

504   THE ONE FATHER

God and Father of all, who made of one blood all nations of men to dwell on the face of the earth:

Deepen our understanding of peoples of other races, languages, and customs than our own.

Teach us to view them in the light of your own all-embracing love and creative purpose.

Give us a vision of the true brotherhood of mankind, united under one Father.

We ask this in the name of him who died that all men might be one, even Jesus Christ our Lord.

(Acts 17: 26)   *Frank Colquhoun*

505   RECONCILIATION IN CHRIST

Lord Jesus Christ, you are yourself our peace,
    for those who were separated you have made to be one
    and have destroyed the barrier between them.
We thank you for the peace which you came to preach
    to those who were far away, and
    to those who were near.
May all who in your body are reconciled to God
    fulfil your purpose
        to create in yourself one new man, and
        to be at peace with each other,
            rejoicing together
                that we have the same access to the Father by
                    the one Spirit, and
                that we are fellow-citizens in God's household.
Grant then that we may continue to be built together
    to become one dwelling in which God lives by his Spirit.

(Eph. 2: 13–22)   *J. C.*

MEN'S RACIAL PREJUDICE 506

Lord God, Creator and Father of us all,
    you have made of one blood all races and nations of men.
Increase among us the spirit
    of sympathy and understanding,
    of tolerance and goodwill;
that the prejudices, arrogance, and pride
        which cause division
            between those of different race or colour
                may be done away,
                and that
all people may live together in unity and peace;
        through Jesus Christ our Lord.

(Acts 17: 26)   *James M. Todd*

WAR

COMBATANTS 507

Lord God almighty, we pray for all who serve
        as combatants or in support groups in war,
        often through decisions they do not understand
        taken by leaders about whom they know little.
Enable the best qualities of a soldier to develop in them—
    discipline, loyalty, and courage,
    a willingness to accept hardship, and
    a readiness to suffer and even to die for others.
Give them also compassion,
        and deliver them from the spirit
        of cruelty or revenge.
Help them to turn to you in the hour of danger
    and in loneliness,
        and to remain faithful to their families at home.
If they find themselves agonizing in conscience
        because of what they are required to do,
    give them a rich measure of the guidance and strength of
    your Holy Spirit,
        that even from the sin of man
        glory may be brought to your name.

                              J. C.

508 ITS VICTIMS

O Saviour Christ, in whom there is
  neither Jew nor Greek,
  East nor West,
  black nor white:
We pray for all, of whatever nation, who suffer
  because of human strife;
    especially for those least able to receive human help;
    those whose hearts are still bitter;
    those whom we remember today. *Bosnia Chechnya*
                                    Rwanda + Burundi
We pray that, through your ministry of love and life, *+ Sudan*
  their wounds of body and spirit may be healed, and
  that in you men may find peace with God and
                              peace with one another;
    for your truth and mercy's sake.

(Col. 3: 11)   C. Idle

509 THE PEACEMAKERS

  O Father of mercies and God of all comfort, whose Son
ministered to those in need:
  Remember for good all who suffer through the wars of men
and nations, by loss of home or faculties, by loss of friends and
loved ones, by loss of happiness or security or freedom.
  Look upon our world, still torn apart by violence and pain,
and grant success to those who work for peace;
  Through him who reconciled us with God, and with one
another, the Lord Jesus Christ.

(Eph. 2: 16–19)   C. Idle

CHRISTIANS IN A TIME OF WAR   510

God of power and love, look in mercy upon our war-torn world, which is still your world. You have made it; in it you delight to work; you have redeemed its people.

By the cross of Christ, grant reconciliation to those who are now at variance or in conflict with one another, and put an end to all hostility.

Let your servants not be troubled by wars and rumours of wars, but rather look up because their redemption draws near, so that when our King returns he may find many waiting for him, and fighting with his weapons alone.

We ask this in the King's name, Jesus Christ your Son our Lord.

(Matt. 24: 6–7; Luke 21: 28; Eph. 2: 16)   *C. Idle*

SPORT

INTERNATIONAL COMPETITION   511

Lord God, we pray for all athletes and sportsmen from many nations who gather in competition.

Enable them to compete freely and fairly, and deliver them from bitterness in their rivalry with each other and between nations.

Grant to all spectators an appreciation of good sportsmanship and a restraint in their reaction to disappointment.

May this gathering contribute to that fellowship among men of different nations whose highest expression is seen when there is no Greek or Jew, slave or free, but Christ is all, and is in all.

(Col. 3: 11)   *J. C.*

STEWARDSHIP

512   THE CHURCH AROUSED

Infinite Lord and eternal God:
    rouse your church in this land;
    restore your people's sense of mission;
    revive your work in power and might;
    teach us to give
        more of our money,
        more of our interest,
        more of our time,
        more of our prayer, and
        more of ourselves;
That your kingdom may be advanced throughout the world.
    In the name of Christ, the Lord.

Michael Saward

513   THE EARTH'S RESOURCES

O God, the only source of life and energy and wealth
    on our planet earth:
Teach us to conserve and not to squander
        the riches of nature;
      to use rightly our heritage
        from former generations; and
      to plan for the welfare of our children's children.
    Renew our wonder at your creation;
    awaken our concern for all you have made;
    make us better stewards, and
    more careful tenants of the world you lend us as our home.
Hear us, O Lord, our creator,
    in the name of Christ, our redeemer.

Timothy Dudley-Smith

PERSONAL RESPONSIBILITY 514

Lord Jesus Christ, you have taught us
   that we cannot love God *and* money, and
   that all our possessions are a trust from you.
Teach us to be faithful stewards of
   our time,
   our talents, and
   our money,
     that we may help others and
      extend your kingdom;
       for your name's sake.

(Matt. 6: 24; Luke 12: 16–21)   *M. H. Botting's collection*

ACKNOWLEDGEMENTS

The editor and publisher gratefully acknowledge permission to reproduce copyright prayers in this volume.

The following list is arranged alphabetically by the ascription given at the foot of each prayer. An asterisk (*) indicates that the prayer has been adapted by the editor for inclusion in this volume.

David Adam: Reprinted by permission of Triangle/SPCK from *The Edge of Glory* by David Adam: 112, 130, *403

Advisory Council for the Church's Ministry (ACCM): Reproduced by kind permission of the Central Board of Finance of the Church of England from *Pray for your Clergy* (CIO Publishing, 1965) and from *Ember Prayers* (ACCM, 1966): *291, 296, 297

Anon. (Isaiah 53: 6; Philippians 3: 10): Reproduced by permission of Lutterworth Press from *Daily Prayer and Praise* by George Appleton: *91

St Anselm: Reproduced by permission of A. R. Mowbray & Co. Ltd., from *Prayers for use at the Alternative Services* by David Silk: 333

St Augustine: Reproduced from ibid.: 330

George Appleton: Reproduced by permission of the author from *Contemporary Parish Prayers* (Hodder & Stoughton, 1974): 51; and reproduced by permission of Lutterworth Press from *Daily Prayer and Praise*: *84

Walter Barker: Reproduced by permission of the Church's Ministry Among the Jews from *Prayers for Today's Church*: 12

Simon H. Baynes: Reproduced by kind permission of the author from Dick Williams, *Prayers for Today's Church*: 55, 176, *233, *410, *497; and from *More Prayers for Today's Church*: 36

Frank M. Best: Reproduced from Dick Williams, *Prayers for Today's Church*: 462

Book of Common Order (1940): Adapted by permission of the Panel of Worship of The Church of Scotland, General Assembly Board of Practice and Procedure: *80

Book of Common Prayer: All rights in the Book of Common Prayer 1662 are vested in the Crown in the United Kingdom and controlled by Royal Letters Patent: *224, *229, *231, *331, *336, *366, *411

A Book of Prayers for Students (SCM Press, 1915): Reproduced by permission of the publisher: *440

Michael Botting: Reproduced by kind permission of the author from *Family Worship*, ed. M. Botting (CPAS, 1971): *31, 40, *116, 127, 137, *225, *385, 442; and from *Contemporary Parish Prayers* (Hodder & Stoughton, 1974): 104, 293, 304

ACKNOWLEDGEMENTS

William Bright: Reproduced from *Prayer by Prayer* by R. J. Eddison (Henry E. Walter Ltd.): *376

Michael Buckley: Reproduced by permission of Hodder & Stoughton from *A Treasury of the Holy Spirit*, © 1981 by Michael Buckley: 143, *358

Ian D. Bunting: Reproduced by kind permission of the author from *Prayers for Today's Church*: *105, 106, *109

Beryl Bye: Reproduced by kind permission of the author from Beryl Bye, *Prayers for All Seasons* (Lutterworth Press): *25, *216, *327, *384, *420

Christian Aid: Reproduced by kind permission from *Caring for God's World*: *347, 496

Frank Colquhoun: Reproduced by permission of Hodder & Stoughton from *Contemporary Parish Prayers*, © 1974 by Frank Colquhoun: 13, *14, *23, 27, 32, *39, 42, *45, 67, *70, *71, 77, 82, 88, *93, 100, 103, 108, 117, *122, *123, 124, 129, *152, 164, 167, 183, 236, 269, 275, 286, 298, *300, 313, 329, 346, *409, 481, 487, 504; and from *New Parish Prayers*, © 1981 by Frank Colquhoun: 97, 126, *192, *193, 196, *214, 226, 234, 239, 295, 323, 325, 340, 351, 352, *353, *365, 380, *417, *425, 439, *458, 485

John Conacher: All prayers having the attribution 'J. C.', together with indexes and tables, are © the author.

Llewellyn Cumings: Reproduced by kind permission of the author: *146, 322, *382, 396

Daily Prayer: Reproduced by permission of Oxford University Press from *Daily Prayer* compiled by Eric Milner-White and G. W. Briggs: 339, 456

Edward Dering: Reproduced by permission of Lutterworth Press from *Daily Prayer and Praise*, edited by George Appleton: *16

Bishop John Dowden: Reproduced from *Prayer by Prayer*, edited by R. J. Eddison (Henry E. Walter Ltd.): *208

Timothy Dudley-Smith: Reproduced by kind permission of the author: 52, 160, 276, 294, *357, *423, *513

John Eddison: Reproduced from *Prayer by Prayer*, edited by J. Eddison by permission of Henry E. Walter Ltd.: 4, 199, 201, *202, 203, *204, *205, 206, 221, 314, *335, *337, 338, 362, 368, *371, *393, 394, 412, 413, 431, *441, 444, 448, *455, *463

Harold E. Evans: Reproduced from *Prayers for Today's Church*, edited by Dick Williams: 121

Joyce Francis: Reproduced by kind permission of the author from *Prayers for Today's Church*: *101

C. M. Gray-Stack: Reproduced by kind permission of Mrs M. Gray-Stack from *Book of Occasional Prayers*: *348, 372

Canon Peter Green: Reproduced from *Prayer by Prayer*, edited by R. J. Eddison (Henry E. Walter Ltd.): *302

Marjorie Hampson: Reproduced by kind permission of the author from *Prayers for Today's Church*, edited by Dick Williams: 388

W. A. Hampson: Reproduced from ibid., by kind permission of Marjorie Hampson: *433

Christopher Idle: Reproduced by kind permission of the author: 20, 166, 168, *189, 209, *306, 341, 374, 379, *387, 391, 416, *429, 437, *445, *454, 457, *471, 508, 509, 510

Thomas à Kempis: Reproduced by permission of A. R. Mowbray & Co. Ltd., from *Prayers for use at the Alternative Services* by David Silk: *443

John Kingsnorth: Reproduced by kind permission of the author and USPG from *Network and Prayers for Mission*: *284; and by kind permission of the author from *Contemporary Parish Prayers*: *289

H. P. Leatherland: Reproduced by permission of A. R. Mowbray & Co. Ltd., from *Prayers for use at the Alternative Services*: 469.

Liturgy of the Reformed Church of France: Reproduced by permission of Hodder & Stoughton from *Contemporary Parish Prayers*, © 1974 by Frank Colquhoun: *133

Liverpool Cathedral: Reproduced from *Prayers for Today's Church*, edited by Dick Williams: *414

St Ignatius Loyola: Reproduced by permission of A. R. Mowbray & Co. Ltd., from *Prayers for use at the Alternative Services*: *180

Peter Markby: Reproduced from *Prayers for Today's Church*: *434

Eric Milner-White: Reproduced by permission of A. R. Mowbray & Co. Ltd., from *After the Third Collect*: *243

Patricia Mitchell: Reproduced by kind permission of the author from *Prayers for Today's Church*: 56, *169, *242, *320, *470

Dwight L. Moody: Reproduced from *Prayer by Prayer*, edited by R. J. Eddison (Henry E. Walter Ltd.): *334

Mothers' Union: Reproduced by permission from *The Mothers' Union Service Book*: 373; and from *The Mothers' Union Prayer Book*: 319, 343, 361

Basil Naylor: Reproduced by kind permission of the author from *New Parish Prayers*: 175

NIV: Scripture quotations marked (NIV) are from the Holy Bible, New International Version. Copyright © 1973, 1978, International Bible Society. Published by Hodder & Stoughton: 244–63, 267, 270

Orders and Prayers for Church Worship: *315, *318, *378

Martin Parsons: Reproduced by kind permission of the author from *New Parish Prayers*: *195

John Poulton: Reproduced by kind permission of the author from *New Parish Prayers*: *408, 482

John Wheatley Price; Reproduced by kind permission of the author: 7, *50, *493

Stanley Pritchard: Reproduced by permission of Hodder & Stoughton from *New Parish Prayers*, © 1981 by Frank Colquhoun: *353

Michael Saward: Reproduced by kind permission of the author from *Task Unfinished: Prayers for Mission*, © Michael Saward 1973: *53, 54, 69, *119, 132, 157, *158, *159, *171, *227, 397, *405, *422, *426, *428, *453, 484, 490, *501, *512

John D. Searle: Reproduced by permission of the author from *More Prayers for Today's Church*: 210; and from *Prayers for Today's Church*: *211

David Silk: Reproduced by permission of A. R. Mowbray & Co. Ltd., from *Prayers for use at the Alternative Services*: 110, 162, 235, 237, 303, 438, 489; and by permission of the publisher from *Response* (adapted by David Silk), Forward Movement Publications, Cincinnati, Ohio, USA: *238

Society of St Luke the Painter: Reproduced from *Prayers for Today's Church*: 311

John R. W. Stott: Reproduced by kind permission of the author: 476

William Temple: Reproduced by permission of Macmillan, London & Basingstoke, on behalf of the Executors of the Estate of William Temple: 222, 287, *421

Kenneth Thornton: Reproduced by kind permission of the author from *Prayers for Today's Church*: *375

R. C. Thorp: Reproduced from *Prayers for Today's Church*: *1

James M. Todd: Reproduced by kind permission of Mrs E. Todd: 506

Jamie Wallace: Reproduced by permission of Hodder & Stoughton from *A Month of Sundays*, © 1983 Jamie Wallace: 57, 62, 64, 139, 142, *177, 218, 230, *240, *264, 265, 268, *386, *474, 475

Andrew C. Warner: Reproduced by kind permission of the author: *26, *400

Alan C. Warren: Reproduced by kind permission of the author: 9, *174

Leslie Weatherhead: Reproduced from *A Private House of Prayer*, by kind permission of the family of Dr Leslie Weatherhead, who own the copyright: 480

Dick Williams: Reproduced by kind permission of the author from *Prayers for Today's Church*: *17, *19, *28, *85, 86, 87, *96, *128, *185, *312, *324, *349, *354, 389, *390, *399, *407, *415, *435, 492; and from *More Prayers for Today's Church*: *10, 18, 125, 460

ACKNOWLEDGEMENTS

Susan Williams: Reproduced from *Prayers for Today's Church*: 47, *48, *66, *79, *342, *383, *418; and from *More Prayers for Today's Church*: 149

D. R. Woodman: Reproduced by permission of Hodder & Stoughton from *Contemporary Parish Prayers*, © 1974 by Frank Colquhoun: *409

Bishop Theodore Woods: Reproduced from *Prayer by Prayer* by R. J. Eddison (Henry E. Walter Ltd.): *198

Bernard Woolf: Reproduced by kind permission of the author from *Prayers for Today's Church*: *173, 369

Worship Now: Reproduced by permission of St Andrew Press from *Worship Now*, compiled by D. Cairns, I. Pitt-Watson, J. A. Whyte, and T. B. Honeyman: *376, 377

ACKNOWLEDGMENTS

INDEX OF TOPICS

The numbers refer to the individual prayers, and not to pages.

INDEX OF SCRIPTURE ALLUSIONS

This is not an exhaustive index of Scripture references contained within the prayers, but it should help in finding a prayer relevant to a reading or to the text of a sermon. Not all gospel parallels are given, nor all references to the narrative portions of the gospels and Acts related to Christmas, Easter, Ascension, and Pentecost.

The numbers refer to the individual prayers, and not to pages.

INDEX OF SCRIPTURE ALLUSIONS

JOHN (*cont.*):

2: 1–11	46, 373, 374, 375, 382
2: 13–16	48
3: 14–18	24, 396, 458
4: 4–14	49
6: 1–14	47
6: 34–5	107
6: 57, 58	107
8: 12	470
8: 36	306
10: 1–18	111, 118
10: 11	110
11: 38–44	115
12: 9–11	115
12: 24–6	76
13: 1–17	88, 430
14: 2, 3	123, 183, 310
14: 6	9, 11, 462
15: 5–7	64
16: 13–15	120
16: 22–4	231, 393
17: 14–18	150
17: 21	287
19: 17	78
19: 30	200
20: 10–19	99
20: 19–23	97, 105, 200, 257, 503
20: 24–9	106
21: 1–12	114

ACTS

2: 17–21	398, 473
2: 38–9	135
3: 16	38
4: 13	221
4: 24–30	163
8: 26–38	140
14: 23	295
14: 26–7	488
15: 31	280
16: 25–34	459
17: 26–7	473, 504, 506
20: 26–35	25, 299
20: 28	117
27: 21–3	419

ROMANS

1: 16	419

4: 13	8
4: 20–5	8
5: 1–11	179
5: 8	178
6: 2–12	76, 190
6: 4	43
6: 22	76
8: 1	21
8: 18	181
8: 19–21	3
8: 28	181
8: 35–9	313, 352
10: 8–15	102
11: 33–6	249
12: 10–18	483
13: 1	446
15: 13	103, 252
16: 3, 9	274

I CORINTHIANS

1: 10–17	273
1: 23–4	273
2: 1–5	273
2: 16	283
4: 1, 2	391
9: 24–5	471
10: 32	305
11: 23–6	82, 90
11: 26–8	273
12: 4–12	278, 288
12: 25	282
13	146, 273
14: 24–6	273
15: 57	195
16: 13, 14	251, 273
16: 23	251

2 CORINTHIANS

1: 1–2	278
1: 3–4	316
2: 5–8	273
3: 11–12	273
4: 4–10	2
5: 17	193, 305
5: 20	2, 177, 273, 491
6: 19–20	68
8: 2–5	273
8: 9	27
13: 11	273

INDEX OF SCRIPTURE ALLUSIONS

INDEX OF SCRIPTURE READINGS

This index refers to all the readings which are printed *in extenso* in the 'Collects and Readings' section of the Alternative Prayer Book 1984; it shows the days on which they are appointed for use, and is intended particularly for use with Section A of this book ('The Church's Year').

Many of the days are shown here in an abbreviated form, which will be understood by reference to the normal conventions. Please note, however, that

'2 b. Christmas' denotes the second Sunday before Christmas
and
'Christmas 2' denotes the second Sunday after Christmas.

	Days in Year 1	*Days in Year 2*
GENESIS		
1: 1–3, 24–31a	9 b. Christmas	
2: 4b–9		9 b. Christmas
2: 7–9	Lent 1	
2: 15–25		9 b. Christmas
3: 1–7	Lent 1	
3: 1–15		8 b. Christmas
4: 1–10	8 b. Christmas	Lent 1
6: 11–22	Lent 2	
7: 17–24		Lent 2
11: 1–9	Pentecost	
12: 1–4	St Thomas	St Thomas
12: 1–9	7 b. Christmas	Lent 3
22: 1–13	Lent 3	
22: 1–18		7 b. Christmas
28: 10–22	Pentecost 19	
32: 22–30		Pentecost 20
45: 1–15		Pentecost 14
EXODUS		
3: 1–6		Lent 4
3: 7–15	6 b. Christmas	
6: 2–8		6 b. Christmas
6: 2–13	Lent 5	
12: 1–14	Maundy Thursday	Maundy Thursday
12: 21–7	Christmas 2	
14: 15–22	Easter	Easter
15: 1–11	Easter 1	
16: 2–15		Easter 1
19: 1–6	Pentecost 2	
19: 16–24		Pentecost
20: 1–17	Pentecost 5	
24: 3–11	Pentecost 6	

EXODUS (*cont.*):	*Days in Year 1*	*Days in Year 2*
33: 12–23	Epiphany 3	
	St John Evangelist	St John Evangelist
34: 29–35	Lent 4	
	Transfiguration	Transfiguration
LEVITICUS		
19: 9–18	Pentecost 16	
NUMBERS		
15: 32–6		Quinquagesima
DEUTERONOMY		
6: 17–25	Pentecost 3	
7: 6–11	Pentecost 4	
8: 1–6		Epiphany 3
8: 1–10	Rogation Tuesday	Rogation Tuesday
8: 11–20		Pentecost 3
10: 12 to 11: 1		Pentecost 7
11: 18–28	Pentecost 22	Pentecost 22
15: 7–11		Pentecost 16
26: 1–11	Pentecost 18	
32: 1–9	St Patrick	St Patrick
34: 1–12		Easter 5
JOSHUA		
1: 1–9	Pentecost 9	
RUTH		
1: 8–17, 22		Pentecost 5
I SAMUEL		
1: 20–8		Christmas 1
2: 27–35	St Matthias	St Matthias
3: 1–10		Epiphany 2
16: 1–13a	Epiphany 1	
17: 37–50		Pentecost 9
24: 9–17		Pentecost 10
2 SAMUEL		
7: 4–16		Pentecost 9
12: 1–10	Epiphany 6	Epiphany 6
I KINGS		
3: 4–15		Pentecost 15
8: 22–30	Epiphany 4	
8: 35–40	Rogation Wednesday	Rogation Wednesday

	Days in Year 1	*Days in Year 2*
17: 17–24	Wednesday in Easter Week	Wednesday in Easter Week
		Easter 3
19: 9–18	5 b. Christmas	
19: 15–21	Conversion St Paul	Conversion St Paul

2 KINGS

2: 1–15		Easter 6
5: 1–14		Sexagesima
6: 8–17	St Michael & All Angels	St Michael & All Angels

1 CHRONICLES

29: 1–9		Pentecost 11

2 CHRONICLES

24: 20–2	St Stephen	St Stephen

NEHEMIAH

6: 1–16		Pentecost 18

JOB

14: 1–14	Easter Eve Saturday in Easter Week	Easter Eve Saturday in Easter Week
28: 1–11	Rogation Monday	Rogation Monday
29: 11–16	St Barnabas	St Barnabas
42: 1–6	Pentecost 10	

PROVERBS

2: 1–9	Epiphany 5	Epiphany 5
3: 1–8		Septuagesima
3: 9–18	St Matthew	St Matthew
4: 10–18	SS Philip & James	SS Philip & James
4: 10–19		Easter 4
15: 28–33	St Mark	St Mark
31: 10–31	Pentecost 14	

ISAIAH

6: 1–8	Pentecost 1	Pentecost 1
7: 10–14	Christmas 1	
9: 2–7	Christmas Day	Christmas Day
9: 2, 6–7	Naming of Jesus	Naming of Jesus
10: 20–3		5 b. Christmas
11: 1–9	1 b. Christmas	
12: 1–6	Easter Day	Easter Day
25: 6–9	Easter 2	
28: 9–16	SS Simon & Jude	SS Simon & Jude
30: 18–21	Septuagesima	

	Days in Year 1	*Days in Year 2*
ISAIAH (*cont.*):		
33: 17–22	Last after Pentecost	Last after Pentecost
35: 3–6	St Luke	St Luke
40: 1–11	2 b. Christmas	
	Birth John Baptist	Birth John Baptist
42: 1–7		Epiphany 1
	Monday in Holy Week	Monday in Holy Week
	Pentecost 11	
42: 10–16	Monday in Easter Week	Monday in Easter Week
43: 16–21	Easter Day	Easter Day
45: 1–7	Pentecost 15	
49: 1–6	Epiphany	Epiphany
	Tuesday in Holy Week	Tuesday in Holy Week
	Pentecost 12	
50: 4–9a	Palm Sunday	Palm Sunday
	Wednesday in Holy Week	Wednesday in Holy Week
	Pentecost 13	
51: 4–11		4 b. Christmas
52: 7–10	4 b. Christmas	
	Annunciation	Annunciation
52: 13 to 53: 12	Good Friday	Good Friday
55: 1–11	3 b. Christmas	
57: 15–21		Quinquagesima
58: 1–8	Ash Wednesday	Ash Wednesday
60: 1–6		Christmas 2
61: 1–7	Easter 3	
61: 4–9	St Bartholomew	St Bartholomew
62: 1–5	Christmas Eve	Christmas Eve
	Easter 4	
62: 10–12	Christmas Day	Christmas Day
63: 7–14		Pentecost 4
64: 1–7		3 b. Christmas
JEREMIAH		
1: 4–10	Epiphany 2	
7: 1–11	Pentecost 17	Epiphany 4
20: 7–11a		Pentecost 13
29: 1, 4–14	Last after Pentecost	
31: 1–14	Thursday in Easter Week	Thursday in Easter Week
31: 15–17	Holy Innocents	Holy Innocents
31: 31–4		Lent 5
	All Saints	All Saints
32: 6–15		Pentecost 17
45: 1–5	St James	St James

INDEX OF SCRIPTURE READINGS

INDEX OF SCRIPTURE READINGS

	Days in Year 1	*Days in Year 2*
JOHN (*cont.*):		
21: 20–5	Saturday in Easter Week	Saturday in Easter Week
	St John Evangelist	St John Evangelist

ACTS

1: 1–11	Ascension	Ascension
1: 15–17	St Matthias	St Matthias
1: 20–6	St Matthias	St Matthias
2: 1–11	Pentecost	Pentecost
2: 37–47		Pentecost 2
4: 8–12		Pentecost 3
	Naming of Jesus	Naming of Jesus
5: 12–16	St Bartholomew	St Bartholomew
7: 54–60	St Stephen	St Stephen
7: 54 to 8: 1	Pentecost 13	
8: 26–38		Pentecost 4
9: 1–22	Conversion St Paul	Conversion St Paul
10: 34–38a	Epiphany 1	
11: 4–18		Pentecost 5
11: 19–30	St Barnabas	St Barnabas
11: 27 to 12: 2	St James	St James
13: 16–25	Christmas Eve	Christmas Eve
13: 16–26	Birth John Baptist	Birth John Baptist
16: 6–12a	St Luke	St Luke
17: 22–34		Pentecost 12
20: 17–35		Pentecost 13
26: 1–8	Pentecost 21	
26: 1, 9–20	Epiphany 2	

ROMANS

1: 18–25	Epiphany 6	Epiphany 6
4: 13–25	7 b. Christmas	
5: 1–11		Pentecost 19
6: 3–11	Pentecost 3	
7: 7–13		8 b. Christmas
8: 1–11		Pentecost 7
8: 11–17	Christmas 2	
8: 18–25	Pentecost 20	
8: 28–39		Easter 5
9: 19–28		5 b. Christmas
10: 12–18	St Andrew	St Andrew
11: 13–24	5 b. Christmas	
12: 1–8		Christmas 1
12: 9–21	Pentecost 16	
13: 1–7	Pentecost 15	
13: 8–14		4 b. Christmas
15: 1–6	St Columba	St Columba
15: 4–13		3 b. Christmas

INDEX OF SCRIPTURE READINGS

INDEX OF SCRIPTURE READINGS

	Days in Year 1	*Days in Year 2*
1 JOHN		
1: 1–4	St Brigid	St Brigid
1: 1–7	Epiphany 3	
2: 1–11	St John Evangelist	St John Evangelist
2: 22–9	Pentecost 22	Pentecost 22
3: 1–10		Lent 2
3: 9–18	8 b. Christmas	
4: 1–6	Lent 2	
4: 7–14	Christmas Day	Christmas Day
4: 15–21		Pentecost 16
5: 12–15	Rogation Wednesday	Rogation Wednesday
REVELATION		
1: 10–18	Easter	Easter
3: 14–22	Easter 4	
4: 1–11		9 b. Christmas
7: 2–4		Last after Pentecost
	All Saints	All Saints
7: 9–17		Last after Pentecost
	All Saints	All Saints
12: 7–12	St Michael & All Angels	St Michael & All Angels
19: 6–9	Easter 2	
21: 1–7		1 b. Christmas
	Birth of Virgin Mary	Birth of Virgin Mary
21: 22 to 22: 5		Christmas 2

CALENDAR

THE table on the two following pages lists the Sundays and major movable feasts in the liturgical year of the Alternative Prayer Book 1984. For each, it shows the date in the calendar year on which it falls.

The days of the week on which Christmas Eve, Christmas Day, and Epiphany occur are also shown.

The information is provided for the period until 18 October 1998.

	1987/88 Year 2 1987	1988/89 Year 1 1988	1989/90 Year 2 1989	1990/91 Year 1 1990	1991/92 Year 2 1991	1992/93 Year 1 1992	1993/94 Year 2 1993	1994/95 Year 1 1994	1995/96 Year 2 1995	1996/97 Year 1 1996	1997/98 Year 2 1997
BEFORE CHRISTMAS											
9TH	25 Oct.	23 Oct.	29 Oct.	28 Oct.	27 Oct.	25 Oct.	24 Oct.	23 Oct.	29 Oct.	27 Oct.	26 Oct.
8TH	1 Nov.	30 Oct.	5 Nov.	4 Nov.	3 Nov.	1 Nov.	31 Oct.	30 Oct.	5 Nov.	3 Nov.	2 Nov.
7TH	8 Nov.	6 Nov.	12 Nov.	11 Nov.	10 Nov.	8 Nov.	7 Nov.	6 Nov.	12 Nov.	10 Nov.	9 Nov.
6TH	15 Nov.	13 Nov.	19 Nov.	18 Nov.	17 Nov.	15 Nov.	14 Nov.	13 Nov.	19 Nov.	17 Nov.	16 Nov.
5TH	22 Nov.	20 Nov.	26 Nov.	25 Nov.	24 Nov.	22 Nov.	21 Nov.	20 Nov.	26 Nov.	24 Nov.	23 Nov.
4TH (Advent 1)	29 Nov.	27 Nov.	3 Dec.	2 Dec.	1 Dec.	29 Nov.	28 Nov.	27 Nov.	3 Dec.	1 Dec.	30 Nov.
3RD (Advent 2)	6 Dec.	4 Dec.	10 Dec.	9 Dec.	8 Dec.	6 Dec.	5 Dec.	4 Dec.	10 Dec.	8 Dec.	7 Dec.
2ND (Advent 3)	13 Dec.	11 Dec.	17 Dec.	16 Dec.	15 Dec.	13 Dec.	12 Dec.	11 Dec.	17 Dec.	15 Dec.	14 Dec.
1ST (Advent 4)	20 Dec.	18 Dec.	24 Dec.	23 Dec.	22 Dec.	20 Dec.	19 Dec.	18 Dec.	24 Dec.	22 Dec.	21 Dec.
CHRISTMAS											
Eve (24 Dec.)	Thur.	Sat.	Sun.	Mon.	Tue.	Thur.	Fri.	Sat.	Sun.	Tue.	Wed.
Day (25 Dec.)	Fri.	Sun.	Mon.	Tue.	Wed.	Fri.	Sat.	Sun.	Mon.	Wed.	Thur.
1ST after	27 Dec.	**1989** 1 Jan.	31 Dec.	30 Dec.	29 Dec.	27 Dec.	26 Dec.	**1995** 1 Jan.	31 Dec.	29 Dec.	28 Dec.
2ND after	**1988** 3 Jan.	—	—	—	**1992** 5 Jan.	**1993** 3 Jan.	**1994** 2 Jan.	—	—	**1997** 5 Jan.	**1998** 4 Jan.
EPIPHANY (6 Jan)	Wed.	Fri.	**1990** Sat.	**1991** Sun.	Mon.	Wed.	Thur.	Fri.	**1996** Sat.	Mon.	Tue.
1ST after	10 Jan.	8 Jan.	7 Jan.	13 Jan.	12 Jan.	10 Jan.	9 Jan.	8 Jan.	7 Jan.	12 Jan.	11 Jan.
2ND after	17 Jan.	15 Jan.	14 Jan.	20 Jan.	19 Jan.	17 Jan.	16 Jan.	15 Jan.	14 Jan.	19 Jan.	18 Jan.
3RD after	24 Jan.	—	21 Jan.	—	26 Jan.	24 Jan.	23 Jan.	22 Jan.	21 Jan.	—	25 Jan.
4TH after	—	—	28 Jan.	—	2 Feb.	31 Jan.	—	29 Jan.	28 Jan.	—	1 Feb.
5TH after	—		4 Feb.		9 Feb.	—	—	5 Feb.	—		—
6TH after			—								
BEFORE EASTER											
9TH (Septuagesima)	31 Jan.	22 Jan.	11 Feb.	27 Jan.	16 Feb.	7 Feb.	30 Jan.	12 Feb.	4 Feb.	26 Jan	8 Feb.
8TH (Sexagesima)	7 Feb.	29 Jan.	18 Feb.	3 Feb.	23 Feb.	14 Feb.	6 Feb.	19 Feb.	11 Feb.	2 Feb.	15 Feb.
7TH (Quinquagesima)	14 Feb.	5 Feb.	25 Feb.	10 Feb.	1 Mar.	21 Feb.	13 Feb.	26 Feb.	18 Feb.	9 Feb.	22 Feb.
Ash Wednesday	17 Feb.	8 Feb.	28 Feb.	13 Feb.	4 Mar.	24 Feb.	16 Feb.	1 Mar.	21 Feb.	12 Feb.	25 Feb.
6TH (Lent 1)	21 Feb.	12 Feb.	4 Mar.	17 Feb.	8 Mar.	28 Feb.	20 Feb.	5 Mar.	25 Feb.	16 Feb.	1 Mar.
5TH (Lent 2)	28 Feb.	19 Feb.	11 Mar.	24 Feb.	15 Mar.	7 Mar.	27 Feb.	12 Mar.	3 Mar.	23 Feb.	8 Mar.
4TH (Lent 3)	6 Mar.	26 Feb.	18 Mar.	3 Mar.	22 Mar.	14 Mar.	6 Mar.	19 Mar.	10 Mar.	2 Mar.	15 Mar.
3RD (Lent 4)	13 Mar.	5 Mar.	25 Mar.	10 Mar.	29 Mar.	21 Mar.	13 Mar.	26 Mar.	17 Mar.	9 Mar.	22 Mar.
2ND (Lent 5) (Passion)	20 Mar.	12 Mar.	1 Apr.	17 Mar.	5 Apr.	28 Mar.	20 Mar.	2 Apr.	24 Mar.	16 Mar.	29 Mar.

	1988	1989	1990	1991	1992	1993	1994	1995	1996	1997	1998
Palm Sunday (Lent 6)	27 Mar.	19 Mar.	8 Apr.	24 Mar.	12 Apr.	4 Apr.	27 Mar.	9 Apr.	31 Mar.	23 Mar.	5 Apr.
Good Friday	1 Apr.	24 Mar.	13 Apr.	29 Mar.	17 Apr.	9 Apr.	1 Apr.	14 Apr.	5 Apr.	28 Mar.	10 Apr.
EASTER											
Eve	2 Apr.	25 Mar.	14 Apr.	30 Mar.	18 Apr.	10 Apr.	2 Apr.	15 Apr.	6 Apr.	29 Mar.	11 Apr.
Day	3 Apr.	26 Mar.	15 Apr.	31 Mar.	19 Apr.	11 Apr.	3 Apr.	16 Apr.	7 Apr.	30 Mar.	12 Apr.
1ST after	10 Apr.	2 Apr.	22 Apr.	7 Apr.	26 Apr.	18 Apr.	10 Apr.	23 Apr.	14 Apr.	6 Apr.	19 Apr.
2ND after	17 Apr.	9 Apr.	29 Apr.	14 Apr.	3 May	25 Apr.	17 Apr.	30 Apr.	21 Apr.	13 Apr.	26 Apr.
3RD after	24 Apr.	16 Apr.	6 May	21 Apr.	10 May	2 May	24 Apr.	7 May	28 Apr.	20 Apr.	3 May
4TH after	1 May	23 Apr.	13 May	28 Apr.	17 May	9 May	1 May	14 May	5 May	27 Apr.	10 May
5TH after	8 May	30 Apr.	20 May	5 May	24 May	16 May	8 May	21 May	12 May	4 May	17 May
ASCENSION	12 May	4 May	24 May	9 May	28 May	20 May	12 May	25 May	16 May	8 May	21 May
1ST after	15 May	7 May	27 May	12 May	31 May	23 May	15 May	28 May	19 May	11 May	24 May
PENTECOST											
Day (Whitsunday)	22 May	14 May	3 June	19 May	7 June	30 May	22 May	4 June	26 May	18 May	31 May
1ST after (Trinity)	29 May	21 May	10 June	26 May	14 June	6 June	29 May	11 June	2 June	25 May	7 June
2ND after (Trinity 1)	5 June	28 May	17 June	2 June	21 June	13 June	5 June	18 June	9 June	1 June	14 June
3RD after (Trinity 2)	12 June	4 June	24 June	9 June	28 June	20 June	12 June	25 June	16 June	8 June	21 June
4TH after (Trinity 3)	19 June	11 June	1 July	16 June	5 July	27 June	19 June	2 July	23 June	15 June	28 June
5TH after (Trinity 4)	26 June	18 June	8 July	23 June	12 July	4 July	26 June	9 July	30 June	22 June	5 July
6TH after (Trinity 5)	3 July	25 June	15 July	30 June	19 July	11 July	3 July	16 July	7 July	29 June	12 July
7TH after (Trinity 6)	10 July	2 July	22 July	7 July	26 July	18 July	10 July	23 July	14 July	6 July	19 July
8TH after (Trinity 7)	17 July	9 July	29 July	14 July	2 Aug.	25 July	17 July	30 July	21 July	13 July	26 July
9TH after (Trinity 8)	24 July	16 July	5 Aug.	21 July	9 Aug.	1 Aug.	24 July	6 Aug.	28 July	20 July	2 Aug.
10TH after (Trinity 9)	31 July	23 July	12 Aug.	28 July	16 Aug.	8 Aug.	31 July	13 Aug.	4 Aug.	27 July	9 Aug.
11TH after (Trinity 10)	7 Aug.	30 July	19 Aug.	4 Aug.	23 Aug.	15 Aug.	7 Aug.	20 Aug.	11 Aug.	3 Aug.	16 Aug.
12TH after (Trinity 11)	14 Aug.	6 Aug.	26 Aug.	11 Aug.	30 Aug.	22 Aug.	14 Aug.	27 Aug.	18 Aug.	10 Aug.	23 Aug.
13TH after (Trinity 12)	21 Aug.	13 Aug.	2 Sept.	18 Aug.	6 Sept.	29 Aug.	21 Aug.	3 Sept.	25 Aug.	17 Aug.	30 Aug.
14TH after (Trinity 13)	28 Aug.	20 Aug.	9 Sept.	25 Aug.	13 Sept.	5 Sept.	28 Aug.	10 Sept.	1 Sept.	24 Aug.	6 Sept.
15TH after (Trinity 14)	4 Sept.	27 Aug.	16 Sept.	1 Sept.	20 Sept.	12 Sept.	4 Sept.	17 Sept.	8 Sept.	31 Aug.	13 Sept.
16TH after (Trinity 15)	11 Sept.	3 Sept.	23 Sept.	8 Sept.	27 Sept.	19 Sept.	11 Sept.	24 Sept.	15 Sept.	7 Sept.	20 Sept.
17TH after (Trinity 16)	18 Sept.	10 Sept.	30 Sept.	15 Sept.	4 Oct.	26 Sept.	18 Sept.	1 Oct.	22 Sept.	14 Sept.	27 Sept.
18TH after (Trinity 17)	25 Sept.	17 Sept.	7 Oct.	22 Sept.	11 Oct.	3 Oct.	25 Sept.	8 Oct.	29 Sept.	21 Sept.	4 Oct.
19TH after (Trinity 18)	2 Oct.	24 Sept.	14 Oct.	29 Sept.	—	10 Oct.	2 Oct.	15 Oct.	6 Oct.	28 Sept.	11 Oct.
20TH after (Trinity 19)	9 Oct.	1 Oct.	—	6 Oct.	—	—	9 Oct.	—	13 Oct.	5 Oct.	—
21ST after (Trinity 20)	—	8 Oct.	—	13 Oct.	—	—	—	—	—	12 Oct.	—
22ND after (Trinity 21)	—	15 Oct.	—	—	—	—	—	—	—	—	—
Last after	16 Oct.	22 Oct.	21 Oct.	20 Oct.	18 Oct.	17 Oct.	16 Oct.	22 Oct.	20 Oct.	19 Oct.	18 Oct.
	1988	**1989**	**1990**	**1991**	**1992**	**1993**	**1994**	**1995**	**1996**	**1997**	**1998**

POSTSCRIPT

THE sad news of Archbishop Armstrong's death has taken my thoughts back to an afternoon in 1971; it was then that he took time to visit my wife and myself at our home in Addis Ababa, although the reason for his coming to Ethiopia was to participate in a conference. I remember his friendly and quiet pastoral interest in what we were doing, the thoughtfulness of his concern as Bishop of Cashel for us as missionaries of the Church of Ireland, and the quality in him which at our first meeting made me glad to find our conversation leading quite easily into confidences which I had shrunk from sharing with any other.

In those days Addis Ababa was almost the cross-roads of Africa, and we were used to having many visitors. I still remember, however, having remarked at the time that I had met no other who had in a short visit shown so full an understanding of the problems of Ethiopia and of the situation and needs of her people.

Dr Armstrong was a man of God who thought carefully, whose judgements were perceptive, and who truly cared for people. He cared in a way that took him far beyond the perfunctory in fulfilling what he regarded as his duty; I saw this in Addis Ababa, and I saw it again in the preparation of *Prayers in Church*.

I knew it to be an honour when I heard that he had agreed to see the typescript of this book, with a view to writing an introduction for it. It was quite a long time afterwards that I had his invitation to go and see him to discuss it. When we met I found that he had not just glanced at it to get a general idea of its nature and contents, but had over many weeks been using it himself in his evening devotions. It was in the light of having done this that he talked over many of the prayers with me, and made the suggestions for improvements that are now incorporated in the book.

Even then, it was to my mind quite remarkable that this humble leader had not merely read the book through but had indeed prayed his way through it. It is a disappointment to me that he will not be with us in mortal form to receive a copy when it is printed. I find it, however, quite moving to be able now to testify that the manner in which he entered so deeply into the preparation of the book means that it can be looked upon as a form of memorial and thanksgiving in the Church for the life and ministry of John Ward Armstrong.

23 July 1987   JOHN CONACHER